OECD Public Governance Reviews

Public Integrity in Ecuador

TOWARDS A NATIONAL INTEGRITY SYSTEM

OECD

BETTER POLICIES FOR BETTER LIVES

This work is published under the responsibility of the Secretary-General of the OECD. The opinions expressed and arguments employed herein do not necessarily reflect the official views of OECD member countries.

This document, as well as any data and map included herein, are without prejudice to the status of or sovereignty over any territory, to the delimitation of international frontiers and boundaries and to the name of any territory, city or area.

Please cite this publication as:
OECD (2021), *Public Integrity in Ecuador: Towards a National Integrity System*, OECD Public Governance Reviews, OECD Publishing, Paris, *https://doi.org/10.1787/9623672c-en*.

ISBN 978-92-64-46624-1 (print)
ISBN 978-92-64-68652-6 (pdf)

OECD Public Governance Reviews
ISSN 2219-0406 (print)
ISSN 2219-0414 (online)

Photo credits: Cover © Ministry of Tourism of Ecuador.

Foreword

Public integrity is the glue that holds societies together. It is the consistent alignment of, and adherence to, shared ethical values, principles and norms for upholding, and prioritising the public interest over private interests in the public sector. Not respecting these values and rules undermines sustainable and inclusive development, and can endanger our democracies. As a key driver of trust in government, public integrity is crucial for ensuring the credibility and therefore the support for and success of policies.

Public integrity is also essential in the current context. Countries are suffering from the consequences of the COVID-19 crisis and have been mobilising significant public resources to make vaccines available, ensure health services, provide support to most vulnerable people and sustain businesses. Unfortunately, this situation has also exacerbated corruption risks, and in many countries corruption cases linked to the management of COVID-19-related resources are adding to citizens' already growing discontent, emphasising the relevance of building a responsive and resilient public integrity system.

To respond to this and other contemporary challenges, Ecuador has recognised the need for continuous improvement of its policies. Although public integrity is a novel issue in the country, Ecuador has showed willingness to develop a national integrity system in line with good international practices and the *OECD Recommendation on Public Integrity* (hereafter "the *OECD Recommendation*"). This will support Ecuador in developing a sustainable answer to corruption, as public integrity aspires to move beyond reacting to scandals only by building a culture of integrity in the whole of government, state and society. Furthermore, it will consolidate Ecuador´s broader efforts to participate in international dialogue – which included joining the OECD Development Centre in 2019 - and to find innovative solutions to promote sustainable and inclusive growth, reduce poverty and inequalities, and improve people's lives.

This report, supported by the German Technical Cooperation in Ecuador, builds on the OECD work and experience on public integrity in Latin America and demonstrates the commitment of the country to raise its integrity standards and practices. It focuses on the institutional and strategic aspects addressed in the first pillar of the *OECD Recommendation*, which Ecuador has identified as priorities in developing an integrity system. As such, the report provides a road map with concrete recommendations which could be considered by the new government elected in 2021 to set the foundations for a comprehensive and strategic approach to integrity. Building on this first report, Ecuador could decide to expand the review to the two other pillars of the *OECD Recommendation* – culture of integrity and accountability – and carry out an OECD Integrity Review, which would enable the country to request adherence to the *OECD Recommendation* as other non-Member countries in the region, such as Argentina and Peru, have done.

Acknowledgements

The report was prepared by the OECD Public Sector Integrity Division of the Directorate of Public Governance under the direction of Elsa Pilichowski, OECD Director for Public Governance and Julio Bacio Terracino, Acting Head of the Public Sector Integrity Division. The report was co-ordinated and drafted by Giulio Nessi of the Public Sector Integrity Division. The report benefitted from the insights and comments from Frédéric Boehm of the Public Sector Integrity Division and from Juan Vazquez Zamora and Cristina Cabutto of the OECD Development Centre. Editorial and administrative assistance was provided by Meral Gedik, Rania Haidar, Andrea Uhrhammer, Laura Uribe, Charles Victor, and Laura Voelker. Laura Córdoba Reyes carried out preliminary research for the report. The Spanish translation of the report was prepared by Carmen Navarrete and edited by the technical team of the Open Government Directorate of the General Secretariat of the Presidency of the Republic of Ecuador.

We thank the financial and technical support given by the German Technical Cooperation, implemented by *Deutsche Gesellschaft für Internationale Zusammenarbeit* (GIZ) GmbH, through the Programme "Ecuador SinCero – Prevention of Corruption, Transparency and Citizen Participation", led by Fiorella Mayaute. In particular Jessica Leguia and Germán Guerra, part of the technical team of Ecuador SinCero, for the support and contributions to the report.

The OECD expresses its gratitude to the Government of Ecuador as well as all the public institutions which took part in the process for their co-operation, in particular the General Secretariat of the Presidency of the Republic (*Secretaría General de la Presidencia de la República*), the Technical Secretariat "Planifica Ecuador" (*Secretaria Técnica Planifica Ecuador*), the Ministry of Labour (*Ministerio del Trabajo*), the Ministry of Health (*Ministerio de Salud Pública*), the Internal Revenue Service (*Servicio de Rentas Internas*), the Ministry of Production, Foreign Trade, Investment and Fisheries (*Ministerio de Producción, Comercio Exterior, Inversiones y Pesca*), the National Public Procurement Service (*Servicio Nacional de Contratación Pública*), the Coordinating Company of Public Companies (*Empresa Coordinadora de Empresas Públicas*), the Ministry of Economy and Finance (*Ministerio de Economía y Finanzas*), the Council for Citizen Participation and Social Control (*Consejo de Participación Ciudadana y Control Social*), the Comptroller General's Office (*Contraloría General del Estado*), the Ombudsman's Office (*Defensoría del Pueblo*), the Technical Secretariat of the Transparency and Control Function´s Coordination Committee (*Secretaría Técnica del Comité Coordinación Función Trasparencia y Control*), the National Assembly (*Asamblea Nacional*), the Judicial Council *(Consejo de la Judicatura)*, and the Municipality of Quito's Metropolitan District (*Municipio del Distrito Metropolitano de Quito*). The OECD would also like to thank the organisations from civil society, private sector and academia which provided valuable insights and perspectives for the elaboration of the report, in particular the Chamber of Commerce of Quito (*Cámara de Comercio de Quito*), the Construction Industry Chamber (*Cámara de la Industria de la Construcción*), Centro Segundo Montes Mozo, Corporación Participación Ciudadana, Fundación Ciudadanía y Desarrollo, Fundación de Ayuda por Internet, Fundación Diálogo Diverso, Fundación Grupo Esquel, Grupo FARO, Instituto de Altos Estudios Nacionales, and the Hemispheres University (*Universidad Hemisferios*). Finally, the General Secretariat of the Presidency of the Republic - in particular Nicolas José Issa Wagner, General Secretary of the Presidency, Ernesto Emilio Varas Valdéz, Undersecretary General of Government Management, María Fernanda Ordoñez Delgado, Undersecretary of Public Administration,

Nelson Sebastián Robelly Alarcón, Open Government Director, and the technical team of the Open Government Directorate - deserves special mention for co-ordinating all the activities, including the virtual fact-finding mission held in December 2020, and the virtual workshops organised in March 2021 where the preliminary recommendations were presented and discussed with representatives from public institutions, civil society, private sector and academia.

This report also benefited from invaluable input provided by OECD peers, in particular Daniella Carizzo, National Civil Service Directorate of Chile (*Dirección Nacional del Servicio Civil*), and Gonzalo Guerrero Valle, Ministry of the Interior and Public Security of Chile (*Ministerio del Interior y Seguridad Pública*).

Table of contents

FIGURES

TABLES

Follow OECD Publications on:

 http://twitter.com/OECD_Pubs

http://www.facebook.com/OECDPublications

http://www.linkedin.com/groups/OECD-Publications-4645871

http://www.youtube.com/oecdilibrary

http://www.oecd.org/oecddirect/

Abbreviations and acronyms

AME	Association of Ecuadorian Municipalities
APEC	Asia-Pacific Economic Cooperation
CAN	High-level Anti-corruption Commission (Peru)
CDE	State Defence Council (Chile)
CELAC	Community of Latin American and Caribbean States
CEPLAN	National Centre for Strategic Planning (Peru)
CGE	Office of the Comptroller General of the State (Ecuador)
CGR	Office of the Comptroller General of the Republic (Chile)
CHILECOMPRA	Public Procurement and Contracting Directorate (Chile)
CMF	Financial Market Commission (Chile)
CNCLCC	National Citizen Commission for the Fight against Corruption (Colombia)
CNM	National Moralization Commission (Colombia)
CONAGOPARE	National council of rural parish governments of Ecuador
CONGOPE	Consortium of provincial autonomous governments (Ecuador)
CPLT	Council for Transparency (Chile)
CSO	Civil Society Organizations
ECU 911	Integrated Security Service (Ecuador)
GAD	Decentralized Autonomous Governments (Ecuador)
GEIRA	Asset Recovery Inter-Agency Liaison Group (Ecuador)
ICAM	Municipal Training Institute (Ecuador)
ICC	International Chamber of Commerce (Ecuador)
ICT	Information and Communications Technology
IDB	Inter-American Development Bank
INMOBILIAR	Public Real Estate Secretariat (Ecuador)
ISO	International Organization for Standardization
JACU	Joint Anti-Corruption Unit (United Kingdom)
LAC	Latin American and the Caribbean
LOSEP	Organic Law of Public Service (Ecuador)
MDMQ	Municipality of the Metropolitan District of Quito (Ecuador)
MESICIC	Mechanism for the Implementation of the Inter-American Convention against Corruption
MINREL	Ministry of Foreign Affairs (Chile)

MINSEGPRES	Public Integrity and Transparency Commission of the Ministry General Secretariat of the Presidency (Chile)
NA	National Assembly of Ecuador
NJS	Higher Hierarchical Level
OAS	Organisation of American States
OECD	Organisation for Economic Co-operation and Development
OII	Institutional Integrity Office (Peru)
PCM	Presidency of the Council of Ministers (Peru)
SDG	Sustainable Development Goals
SENPLADES	National Secretariat for Planning and Development (Ecuador)
SERCOP	National Public Procurement Service (Ecuador)
SIP	Secretariat of Public Integrity (Peru)
ST	Secretariat of Transparency (Colombia)
UAF	Financial Analysis Unit (Chile)
UAFE	Financial and Economic Analysis Unit (Ecuador)
UATH	Human Talent Management Unit (Ecuador)
UNCAC	United Nations Convention Against Corruption
UNODC	United Nations Office on Drugs and Crime
UNDP	United Nations Development Programme
UTA	Transparency and Anti-Corruption Unit (Paraguay)

Executive summary

Similar to other countries in the region and around the world, citizens in Ecuador consider corruption as one of the most crucial challenges of the country and their trust in government has almost halved between 2009 and 2018 according to the results of the Latinobarómetro surveys. Promoting integrity in the public sector is a necessary condition for responding to corruption and reversing this decline of trust. Currently, however, the institutional responsibilities for promoting integrity in Ecuador are fragmented and not clearly assigned. Furthermore, no mechanisms are in place to co-operate and define common goals and actions among institutions, resulting in a lack of a comprehensive strategy and vision to effectively address corruption. Rather than mainstreaming a preventive approach throughout the public sector, existing policies mostly focus on sanctioning corruption and do not address underlying systemic challenges.

Key findings

In Ecuador, integrity-related responsibilities are assigned to various institutions belonging to the five branches – or functions (*funciones*) – of the state. While some co-operation mechanisms are in place among institutions within the same branch and others have been developed among institutions from different branches on enforcement, there are currently no formal or informal arrangements that enable comprehensive co-operation on corruption prevention by bringing together all relevant actors and allowing a dialogue with civil society.

Ecuador has defined some integrity-related objectives in the National Development Plan 2017-2021 and has developed the Public Integrity and Anti-corruption Plan 2019-2023. However, neither plan has brought Ecuador closer to a strategic, comprehensive approach to integrity. The former could not achieve its integrity objectives because it was not accompanied by continuous follow-up activities and monitoring of progress. While identifying some key areas for public integrity, the latter lacks ownership and commitment outside the Transparency and Social Control branch, which developed the Plan. Therefore, its uptake remains limited, especially from the executive branch.

The fragmented institutional context has also hampered the development of an integrity system within the executive branch, where leadership for the integrity and anti-corruption agenda has been passed from one secretariat to another over the last few years. Most recently, the Anti-corruption Secretariat created in 2019 was dissolved a year later without any formal handover of its competences and responsibilities to any other institution. In addition to a lack of institutional leadership and continuity on public integrity, the role of other key integrity actors is undervalued, especially that of the Ministry of Labour. Indeed, this ministry is responsible for a broad range of relevant policy areas, including meritocracy, professionalisation, capacity building, organisational culture, change management, control of the public service and disciplinary enforcement.

Furthermore, laws and policies supporting public integrity at the organisational level, such as managing conflict of interest, whistleblowing or integrity risk-management, are unevenly implemented in the executive branch and do not follow a preventive approach aimed at building organisational cultures of integrity.

Key recommendations

Considering the institutional set-up of the country and experience in other policy areas, Ecuador could establish a National Integrity and Anti-corruption System, led by the President of the Republic and bringing together relevant institutions from all branches of the state and sub-national entities. This mechanism should enable continuous co-operation and ensure the ownership of all actors in the design and implementation of integrity and anti-corruption policies. Learning from past experiences, this system should build on a dialogue phase among all relevant actors, including civil society and the private sector, which would ensure its legitimacy as well as the ownership and commitment of all institutions. Ecuador could take the opportunity to include the development of such a system as one of the priority objectives on public integrity in the National Development Plan 2021-2025.

The National Development Plan 2021-2025 could also define a roadmap leading towards a National Integrity and Anti-corruption Strategy for the 2023-2026 term. This roadmap could include two sequenced steps: first, drafting an Action Plan to implement some key priority actions of the current Public Integrity and Anti-corruption Plan 2019-2023; and, second, developing the new Strategy for the 2023-2026 term following a participative and inclusive co-creation methodology. The recommended National Integrity and Anti-corruption System should lead these efforts to ensure participation, contribution and ownership of all relevant actors in its design and implementation.

In addition, Ecuador could consider the development of a long-term state policy on integrity and anti-corruption to fulfil the constitutional anti-corruption duties of the state as well as to contribute to the implementation of Sustainable Development Goal no. 16 and other integrity and anti-corruption international commitments. This long-term policy would provide a public integrity vision for Ecuador and further address the challenges of institutionalisation, continuity and sustainability of the current integrity and anti-corruption policies.

Finally, Ecuador could define clear integrity responsibilities within the executive branch by leveraging the roles and strengths of the existing institutional context. First, the General Secretariat of the Presidency of the Republic could be responsible for leading and co-ordinating the integrity agenda across the executive and for advising the President of the Republic on public integrity and corruption prevention issues. Given the leading role envisaged for the President as head of the National Integrity and Anti-corruption System, this would allow to ensure the coherence between the strategy set at the national level for all state´s branches and the initiatives taken within the executive branch. The mandate of the General Secretariat of the Presidency should be limited to integrity and corruption prevention only, and not include any tasks related to detection or investigation of possible corruption cases.

At the same time, Ecuador could enhance the role of the Ministry of Labour by assigning it a clear mandate to promote, support and mainstream a culture of public integrity within all the public institutions and entities of the executive branch. Indeed, the Ministry of Labour co-ordinates the human resources units as well as the organisational change and culture units of all public entities. It also manages integrity-related policies such as the code of ethics, conflict of interest, organisational culture, change management, training and disciplinary enforcement. In this context, the organisational change and culture units, whose functions include improving the organisational culture at the entity level, could lead the promotion of a culture of integrity in co-ordination and coherence with the work of the existing Ethics and Anti-corruption Committees, which could maintain their focus on detecting and assessing integrity breaches.

1 Introduction

This Chapter provides an introduction to the report. It highlights the growing perception and impact of corruption among citizens in Ecuador and its effects on the level of trust in government. The Chapter also illustrates the functions of the OECD and how it can support Ecuador in developing a sustainable response to corruption through its integrity standards and extensive regional experience.

Ecuador, similarly to other countries in the Latin American and Caribbean (LAC) region, experiences a growing disconnection between citizens and public institutions, which is also due to the high level of perceived corruption among citizens as well as to the dissatisfaction with such institutions (OECD, 2019[1]) (OECD et al., 2019[2]). Results from the 2018 survey from Latinobarómetro show that the level of trust in governments in the region halved in the last ten years, and that the rate in Ecuador (25%) is sensibly lower than the one registered in 2009 (46.5%) and just above the regional average (22%). At the same time, it highlights that 8% of Ecuadorians perceive corruption as the country's most important problem and more than half of them consider that the level of corruption grew compared to the previous year. Similar findings emerge from the 2018 "Global Corruption Barometer" enquiring direct experiences of corruption in public services and perceptions of the extent of corruption, which reports that 44% of Ecuadorian respondents declared to have paid a bribe to access basic services. These findings are coherent with those of the Americasbarometer showing that, in 2019, 26.6% of respondents reported having been victims of an act of corruption and a growing tolerance for corruption – especially among the young generations - whereas 25% of Ecuadorians justified paying a bribe in certain circumstances, which marks a 12% increase compared to 2014 (Moncagatta et al., 2020[3]; OECD, forthcoming[4]). Corruption has remained one of the highest concerns of Ecuadorian citizens even during the COVID-19 pandemic. A poll conducted in December 2020 highlighted that citizens consider it the third most significant challenge in the country, above the concerns related to the control of COVID-19 but after poverty and unemployment, which corruption contributes to worsen (CEDATOS, 2020[5]).

In Ecuador, in line with the approach of other countries in the region, the anti-corruption efforts have been focused on investigations and sanctions. While being crucial to avoid impunity and ensure the rule of law, this has not proved to be sufficiently effective in controlling corruption. Indeed, the OECD experience shows that a strategic and sustainable response to corruption should be based on public integrity, which refers to the "consistent alignment of, and adherence to, shared ethical values, principles and norms for upholding and prioritising the public interest over private interests in the public sector" (OECD, 2017[6]). This implies that public officials not only comply with the minimum required by law, but that they behave according to the values and standards of conduct inspired by the prominence of the public interest. Public integrity, in turn, creates confidence among citizens and businesses that they live and work in a context of equality of conditions, where meritocracy and efforts, rather than connections or bribes, determine opportunities. Ensuring that values and standards of conduct in the public sector are implemented effectively is therefore a necessary condition for reversing the decline of trust in government, making integrity one of the key levers of trust (Murtin et al., 2018[7]). On the contrary, the erosion of trust undermines the legitimacy of governments and their ability to finance and deliver good quality public services, creating a vicious cycle that further affects citizen satisfaction, erodes the social contract and undermines productivity and sustainable, inclusive economic growth.

The OECD provides countries with a vision for a public integrity strategy, shifting the focus from ad hoc integrity policies to a context dependent, behavioural, risk-based approach with an emphasis on cultivating a culture of integrity across the whole of government and society. For this purpose, based on the experience of OECD member States and research, it adopted the *Recommendation on Public Integrity* consisting of thirteen principles organised in three pillars (Box 1.1). The first pillar focus on how to build a coherent and comprehensive system of public integrity, which requires the commitment of senior public officials but also the clarification of responsibilities and the adoption of a strategic approach. The second pillar promotes the development of a culture of public integrity, which includes capacity-building efforts, merit-based human resources processes, efforts towards an open organisational culture, and a whole-of-society perspective to public integrity. Finally, the third pillar of the Recommendation calls for the establishment of accountability mechanisms through risk management, internal and external audit, disciplinary and criminal enforcement as well as citizen participation and integrity in the decision-making processes.

On top of the Recommendation on Public Integrity, the OECD has adopted other legal instruments related to enhancing integrity and preventing corruption, which are:

- *OECD Recommendation on Guidelines for Managing Conflict of Interest in the Public Service* (OECD, 2004[8]).
- *Recommendation of the Council on Principles for Transparency and Integrity in Lobbying* (OECD, 2010[9]).

Box 1.1. The pillars and components of the *OECD Recommendation on Public Integrity*

I. BUILD A COHERENT AND COMPREHENSIVE PUBLIC-INTEGRITY SYSTEM

1. Demonstrate commitment at the highest political and management levels within the public sector to enhance public integrity and reduce corruption.
2. Clarify institutional responsibilities across the public sector to strengthen the effectiveness of the public integrity system.
3. Develop a strategic approach for the public sector that is based on evidence and aimed at mitigating public integrity risks.
4. Set high standards of conduct for public officials.

II. CULTIVATE A CULTURE OF PUBLIC INTEGRITY

5. Promote a whole-of-society culture of public integrity, partnering with the private sector, civil society, and individuals.
6. Invest in integrity leadership to demonstrate a public sector organisation's commitment to integrity.
7. Promote a merit-based, professional, public sector dedicated to public service values and good governance.
8. Provide sufficient information, training, guidance and timely advice for public officials to apply public integrity standards in the workplace.
9. Support an open organisational culture within the public sector responsive to integrity concerns.

III. ENABLE EFFECTIVE ACCOUNTABILITY

10. Apply an internal control and risk management framework to safeguard integrity in public sector organisations.
11. Ensure that enforcement mechanisms provide appropriate responses to all suspected violations of public integrity standards by public officials and all others involved in the violations.
12. Reinforce the role of external oversight and control within the public integrity system.
13. Encourage transparency and stakeholders' engagement at all stages of the political process and policy cycle to promote accountability and the public interest.

Source: OECD (2017[6]), *OECD Recommendation on Public Integrity*, OECD, Paris, http://www.oecd.org/gov/ethics/Recommendation-Public-Integrity.pdf.

This report focuses on the first pillar of the *OECD Recommendation on Public Integrity* and analyses the general institutional set-up of the main integrity actors in Ecuador in view of their legal mandates, their capacities and their role and responsibilities in integrity policy making, implementation and enabling accountability. The second section addresses the extent to which the relevant actors at the national level have established effective co-operation mechanisms and a strategic approach to public integrity. The third section focuses on the institutional arrangements and responsibilities for integrity within the Executive branch and how they enable implementation of integrity policies at the entity level. Finally, the last section proposes an action plan including all the recommendations of the report and specifying responsible entity(ies) for their implementation.

The aim of the report is to support Ecuador in laying the institutional foundations to establish integrity systems at national level as well as within the Executive branch and its entities. Furthermore, it provides the basis for a more in-depth review of specific policy areas that are introduced in the report and could benefit from additional analysis and recommendations.

The report builds on the analytical framework of the *OECD Recommendation on Public Integrity* and is informed by international good practices, especially from countries with similar legal and institutional set-up in the LAC region with whom the OECD has been working closely through other reviews and the OECD-IDB Network for Integrity in Latin America and the Caribbean (Box 1.2). Furthermore, it benefitted from the extensive information, data and feedback provided by almost 30 national actors between institutions, entities, academia and organisations from civil society and private sector through a questionnaire (October 2020), virtual fact-finding mission interviews (December 2020 - January 2021) and validation workshops (March 2021).

Box 1.2. OECD integrity work and network in the LAC Region

OECD Integrity Reviews

The following OECD Integrity Reviews have been carried out in the LAC region, both at the national and subnational level:

- Argentina (2019)
- Mexico City (2019)
- Nuevo León, Mexico (2018)
- Colombia (2017)
- Coahuila, Mexico (2017)
- Mexico (2017)
- Peru (2017)
- Brazil (2012)

OECD-IDB Network for Integrity in Latin America and the Caribbean

The OECD-IDB Public Integrity Network for Latin America and the Caribbean was launched in 2017, bringing together the main actors responsible for integrity systems in the countries of the region. This includes bodies exclusively dedicated to integrity policies, but also actors responsible for government transparency, public service and internal control. The Network aims to lead policy debates for the exchange of best practices and lessons learned from the implementation of integrity policies at regional and international level. The last meeting was held virtually in September 2020 and focused on the topic "Integrity and transparency in infrastructure projects in times of COVID-19".

Source: OECD (n.d.[10]), "Public Integrity in Latin America and the Caribbean", OECD, Paris, https://www.oecd.org/governance/ethics/integrity-lac.htm (accessed on 12 April 2021).

The OECD is an international organisation made of 38 member States that works to promote policies that foster prosperity, equality, opportunity and well-being for all. Together with governments, policy makers and citizens, it works on establishing evidence-based international standards and finding solutions to a range of governance, social, economic and environmental challenges. It provides a unique forum and knowledge hub for data and analysis, exchange of experiences, best-practice sharing, advice on public policies and international standard-setting (Box 1.3).

Box 1.3. The standard-setting and policy support function of the OECD

- OECD standards are developed by expert committees developed through a rigorous evidence-based process building on best policies and practices and involving a variety of stakeholders.

- OECD standards help to level the global playing field, deepen international technical co-operation, and implement shared policy objectives to improve citizen well-being. Standards create efficiency savings for governments and ensure that policies benefit citizens.

- The OECD has developed over 450 legal instruments (International Agreements, Decisions, Recommendations, Declarations) with currently more than 250 in force, some relating to multiple sectoral areas.

- OECD standards have a truly global reach. For example, the Global Forum on Transparency and Exchange of Information for Tax Purposes has 161 members (including 88 developing countries) working together on implementing tax transparency standards.

- Based on standards and evidence-based analysis, the OECD supports individual countries in their policy reform objectives.

Source: OECD (n.d.[11]), "About the OECD", https://www.oecd.org/about/ (accessed on 12 April 2021).

---

2 Laying the foundations of a national integrity system in Ecuador

This Chapter describes the responsibilities of key national actors with integrity-related functions in Ecuador, which are assigned to different branches of the State. It illustrates the co-operation mechanisms set up between them, and how the creation of a National Integrity and Anti-corruption System could address their limits and enable national dialogue and co-operation across state´s branches and levels of administration on public integrity. The Chapter also analyses the integrity objectives which have been formulated in the National Development Plan 2017-2021 and in the National Public Integrity and Anti-corruption Plan 2019-2023 but have not generated the expected impact. It thus considers how to develop, in a progressive and participative manner, a strategic approach steered by the National Integrity and Anti-corruption System and leading to a long-term integrity vision for Ecuador.

Promoting strategic co-operation between all national integrity actors

Institutional responsibilities on public integrity are assigned to different actors across the five-state branches

An integrity system, whether at the country (national and sub-national) or organisational level, includes different actors with responsibilities for defining, supporting, controlling and enforcing public integrity. While the institutional arrangements to define and assign such responsibilities depend on the institutional and jurisdictional setup of a country, a set of functions should be part of an integrity system according to the OECD *Recommendation on Public Integrity* (Table 2.1).

Table 2.1. Integrity functions

System	Culture	Accountability
• Assigning clear responsibilities. • Ensuring mechanisms to support horizontal and vertical co-operation. • Designing and implementing the integrity strategy or strategies. • Monitoring and evaluating the integrity strategy or strategies. • Setting integrity standards.	• Integrating integrity into human resource management (e.g. assessing the fairness of reward and promotion systems) and personnel management (e.g. integrity as criterion for selection, evaluation and career promotion). • Building capacity and raising the awareness of public officials. • Providing advice and counselling. • Implementing measures to cultivate an open organisational culture. • Opening channels and implementing mechanisms for complaints and whistle-blower protection. • Raising integrity awareness in society. • Conducting civic education programmes. • Implementing measures to support integrity in companies. • Implementing measures to support integrity in civil society organisations.	• Assessing and managing integrity risks. • Applying internal audit. • Implementing enforcement mechanisms. • Applying independent oversight and audit. • Applying access to information and implementing open government measures. • Engaging stakeholders across the policy cycle. • Preventing and managing conflict of interest. • Implementing integrity measures for lobbying. • Implementing integrity measures in financing political parties and election campaigns.

Source: OECD (2020[12]), *OECD Public Integrity Handbook*, OECD Publishing, Paris, https://doi.org/10.1787/ac8ed8e8-en.

In Ecuador, these responsibilities are assigned to various institutions belonging to five branches – also known as functions (*funciones*) of the state – which are the Executive, Legislative, Judicial, Electoral as well as the Transparency and Social Control branches, in line with the separation of powers set in the national Constitution (*Constitución de la República del Ecuador*). The President of the Republic is the head of the State and in charge of the whole public sector (Figure 2.1).

Figure 2.1. Overview of the five state branches of Ecuador

President of the Republic

- The President of the Republic is the Head of State and Government, performs the duties of the Executive Branch of Government.
- The President is also in charge of public administration, which consists of:
  - The bodies and agencies of the Executive, Legislative, Judicial, Electoral and Transparency and Social Control branches.
  - The entities that make up the decentralised autonomous regime.
  - The agencies and entities created by the Constitution or the law for the exercise of State authority, for the provision of public services or to develop economic activities undertaken by the State.
  - The legal persons created by normative act of the decentralised autonomous governments for the provision of public services.

Legislative branch	Executive branch	Judicial and indigenous justice branch	Transparency and Social Control branch	Electoral branch
• The Legislative Branch of Government is exercised by the National Assembly, which is comprised of Assembly persons elected for a four-year term of office. • The National Assembly consists of one single house of representatives and shall have its seat in Quito.	• The President of the Republic performs the duties of the Executive Branch of Government and is the Head of State and Government and is in charge of public administration. • The Executive Branch is comprised of the Office of the President and the Office of the Vice-President of the Republic, the Ministries of State and the other organisations and institutions needed to fulfill, in the framework of their competence, the attributions of Leadership, planning, implementation and evaluation of national public policies and plans that are created to implement them.	• The Judicial Branch is comprised of jurisdictional bodies, administrative bodies, support bodies and autonomous bodies. • The jurisdictional bodies are: 1. The National Court of Justice; 2. The provincial courts of justice; 3. The courts and tribunals provided for by law; 4. The justices of the peace. • The Judiciary Council is the body for the governance, administration, surveillance and discipline of the Judicial Branch. • The Office of the Attorney for the Defense of the People and the Attorney-General's Office are the autonomous bodies of the Judicial Branch.	• The Transparency and Social Control Branch of Government shall promote and foster monitoring of public entities and bodies and of natural persons or legal entities of the private sector who provide services or carry out activities for the general welfare, so they shall conduct them with responsibility, transparency and equity; it shall foster and encourage public participation; it shall protect the exercise and fulfillment of rights; and it shall prevent and combat corruption. • The Transparency and Social Control Branch shall be comprised of the Council for Public Participation and Social Control, the Office of the Human Rights Ombudsman, the Office of the Comptroller General, and the Superintendencies. These entities shall have a legal status and administrative, financial, budgetary and organisational autonomy.	• The Electoral Branch of Government shall guarantee the exercise of political rights as expressed by voting, as well as those referring to the political organisation of the citizenry. • The Electoral Branch shall be comprised of the National Electoral Council and the Electoral Dispute Settlement Court. Both bodies shall have their seat in Quito and shall have national jurisdiction, administrative, financial, and organisational autonomy, and their own legal status. They shall be governed by the principles of autonomy, independence, publicity, transparency, equity, interculturalism, gender equality, swiftness and rectitude.

Source: National Assembly of Ecuador (2008[13]), Constitution of Ecuador, https://www.asambleanacional.gob.ec/sites/default/files/documents/old/constitucion_de_bolsillo.pdf (accessed on 12 April 2021).

Executive branch

In the Executive branch, the anti-corruption and integrity function has been assigned to various specialised anti-corruption bodies that have succeeded in the past years. (Box 3.1). Most recently, in 2019, the Anti-corruption Secretariat (*Secretaría Anticorrupción*) was created through the Executive Decree No. 665 of February 6, 2019 with the following responsibilities:

- Proposing guidelines for the development of public policies and actions that facilitate the report of high-impact acts of corruption committed in the public administration.
- Monitoring the actions against corruption committed in the public administration.
- Mainstreaming the implementation of anti-corruption policies within the Central Government entities.
- Establishing co-operation between government institutions, control agencies, judicial entities and all those involved in the investigation, prosecution and punishment of acts of corruption respecting the division of powers.
- Approving instruments for the systematisation and delivery of supplies or official documentation to the competent bodies through a corresponding route for the fight against corruption.
- Articulating with the Ministry of Foreign Affairs the implementation of existing international agreements that have been acquired by Ecuador in favour of the fight against corruption.
- Proposing to the President of the Republic anti-corruption initiatives.

The Anti-corruption Secretariat was dissolved with the Executive Decree No. 1065 of May 21, 2020 and, although no entity has formally succeeded in its functions, the General Secretariat of the Presidency (*Secretaría General de la Presidencia*) has been promoting public integrity initiatives as part of its work on open government issues.

Next to the Presidency, the Ministry of Labour (*Ministerio del Trabajo*) has key competences in Ecuador integrity system as it is responsible for policies on employment and human resources in the public sector, including recruitment, promotions, capacity building and disciplinary aspects.

From a whole-of-society perspective to public integrity, another key actor is the Ministry of Education (*Ministerio de Educación*), which guarantees access and quality of primary and secondary education and could build a greater role in Ecuador's public integrity system by raising awareness on public integrity and promoting values and knowledge on the exercise of citizenship in Ecuador.

Another relevant institution within the Executive is the Financial and Economic Analysis Unit (*Unidad de Análisis Financiero y Económico*, UAFE), an autonomous technical entity of the Ministry of Economy and Finance (*Ministerio de Economía y Finanzas*), which is responsible for the collection of information, reporting, as well as for the implementation of policies and national strategies for the prevention and identification of money laundering and crimes financing.

Transparency and Social Control branch

The Transparency and Social Control branch of Ecuador (*Función de Transparencia y Control Social*) is entrusted by the Constitution to promote and encourage the control of public sector entities and bodies, as well as natural or legal persons from the private sector that provide services or carry out activities of public interest, so that they perform them with responsibility, transparency, and equity. Its mandate also includes the promotion and encouragement of citizen participation; to protect the exercise and fulfilment of rights; and to prevent and fight corruption. Most relevant responsibilities are:

- Formulate public policies on transparency, control, accountability, promotion of citizen participation and the prevention and fight against corruption.
- Co-ordinate the action plan of the entities of the Transparency and Social Control branch (*plan de acción de las entidades de la Función de Transparencia y Control Social*), without affecting their autonomy.
- Articulate the formulation of the national anti-corruption plan.
- Submit to the National Assembly (*Asamblea Nacional*) proposals for legal reforms within the scope of their competencies.
- Report annually to the National Assembly the activities related to the fulfilment of its functions, or when it requires it to do so.

The Transparency and Social Control branch is formed by institutions, to which the Constitution assigns relevant duties and responsibilities for Ecuador's public integrity system. They are the Council for Citizen Participation and Social Control (*Consejo de Participación Ciudadana y Control Social*), the Ombudsman's Office (*Defensoria del Pueblo*), the Comptroller General's Office (*Contraloría General del Estado*) and the Superintendencies (*Superintendencias*) (Table 2.2).

Table 2.2. Institutions of Ecuador's Transparency and Social Control branch

Actor	Mandate and key functions

Council of Citizen Participation and Social Control (*Consejo de Participación Ciudadana y Control Social*)	• It promotes and encourages the exercise of the rights involving public participation, promotes and sets up social control mechanisms in matters of general welfare, and designates the authorities that pertain to it in accordance with the Constitution and the law. The Council is comprised of seven standing council members and seven alternates.
	• It has the following duties and responsibilities:
	  ○ Promote public participation, encourage public deliberation processes and foster citizenship training, values, transparency, and the fight against corruption.
	  ○ Establish mechanisms for the accountability of public sector institutions and entities and contribute to citizen oversight and social monitoring processes.
	  ○ Urge the other entities of the branch to act obligatorily on matters that merit intervention in the opinion of the Council.
	  ○ Investigate reports about deeds or omissions affecting public participation or leading to corruption.
	  ○ Issue reports that point to evidence of liability, to draft the necessary recommendations and to promote the corresponding legal proceedings.
	  ○ Act as a procedural party in cases filed as consequence of its investigations. When a ruling determines that, in the perpetration of crime, there was improper appropriation of resources, the competent authority shall proceed to seize the personal assets of the sentenced party.
	  ○ Contribute to the protection of citizens who report acts of corruption.
	  ○ Request from any of the entities or officials of State institutions information that it deems necessary for its investigations or proceedings. The citizens and institutions shall co-operate with the Council and those who refuse to do so shall be punishable by law.
	  ○ Organise the process and oversee the transparency in the implementation of the activities of citizen commissions for the selection of state authorities. Designate the head of the Office of the Attorney General (*Procuraduría General del Estado*) and the Superintendencies from among the shortlists proposed by the President of the Republic, after the corresponding citizen challenge and oversight process.
	  ○ Designate the head of the Ombudsman Office (*Defensoría del Pueblo*), the Office of the Public Defender (*Defensoría Pública*), the Office of the Prosecutor General (*Fiscalía General del Estado*), and the Office of the Comptroller General (*Contraloría General del Estado*), after completing the corresponding selection process.
	  ○ Designate the members of the National Electoral Council (*Consejo Nacional Electoral*), the Electoral Dispute Settlement Court (*Tribunal Contencioso Electoral*), and the Judicial Council (*Consejo de la Judicatura*), after completing the corresponding selection process.

Comptroller General of the State (*Contraloría General del Estado*)	• The Office of the Comptroller General is a technical body in charge of controlling the use of State resources and the achievement of the goals of State institutions and private-law legal entities that dispose of government resources.
	• Its functions include to:
	  ○ Direct the administrative control system, comprised of internal auditing, external auditing and internal monitoring of public sector institutions and those private-sector entities that dispose of government resources.
	  ○ Determine administrative and civil liabilities of neglect and gather evidence of criminal liability, related to those aspects and activities subject to its control, without detriment to the duties that, in this matter, pertaining to the Office of the Prosecutor General.
	  ○ Issue regulations for the fulfilment of its functions.
	  ○ Advise State bodies and entities when requested to do so.

Superintendencies (*Superintendencias*)	• They are technical bodies of surveillance, auditing, intervention, and monitoring of economic, social, and environmental activities and of the services provided by public and private entities, for the purpose of ensuring that these activities and services comply with the provisions of the legal system and work for the public interest.
1. of companies, securities and insurance (*de Compañías, Valores y Seguros*)	• Carries out the surveillance, audit, intervention, control and supervision of the securities market, the insurance regime and the non-financial private law legal entities.
2. of banks (*de Bancos*)	• Carries out the surveillance, audit, intervention, control and supervision of financial activities performed by public and private entities of the National Financial System.
3. of popular and solidary economy (*de Economía Popular y Solidaria*)	• Supervises and controls the organisations of the Popular and Solidarity Economy in search of its stability and correct functioning for the welfare of its members and the community in general.

Actor	Mandate and key functions
4. of control of market power (de Control de Poder del Mercado)	• Controls and monitors the correct functioning of the market through the prevention, correction, elimination and/or sanction of the abuse of economic operators with market power, (…), promoting competition, efficiency and transparency of the market and fair trade with the active participation of citizens.
5. of territorial planning, land management and land use (de Ordenamiento Territorial, Uso y Gestión del Suelo)	• Monitors and controls the territorial ordering processes of all levels of government, and the use and management of land, habitat, human settlements and urban development.
6. of information and communication (de Información y Comunicación)	• Guarantee access and exercise of the rights of people to receive truthful, objective, timely, plural, contextualised information, and, to a free, intercultural, inclusive, diverse and participatory communication in all areas, through surveillance, audit, intervention and control of compliance with the regulations.

Ombudsman's Office (Defensoría del Pueblo)	• It has the duty to protect and guarantee the rights of citizens. For that purpose, it has the competence to:
	  ○ Support the actions of protection, habeas corpus, access to public information, habeas data, noncompliance, citizen action and complaints about poor quality or improper provision of public or private services.
	  ○ Issue measures of mandatory and immediate compliance for the protection of rights and to request trial and punishment from the competent authority for their violations.
	  ○ Investigate and rule, in the framework of its attributions, on the deeds or omissions of citizens or legal entities that provide public services.
	  ○ Exercise and promote surveillance of due process of law and immediately prevent and stop all forms of cruel, inhumane and degrading treatment.

Source: National Assembly of Ecuador (2008[13]), Constitution of Ecuador, https://www.asambleanacional.gob.ec/sites/default/files/documents/old/constitucion_de_bolsillo.pdf (accessed on 12 April 2021).

Legislative branch

Other institutions with integrity-related responsibilities belong to other branches of the State. In the Legislative branch, the functions of the National Assembly include the supervision of the acts of the Executive, Electoral and Transparency and Social Control branches, and of the other organs of public power, as well as to request public officials the information it considers necessary.

Judicial branch

Within the Judicial branch, whose governing body is the Judicial Council (Consejo de la Judicatura), the Office of the Prosecutor General (Fiscalía General) directs pre-trial investigations and criminal proceedings, bringing and sustaining cases in front of judges. Within the Office, two Specialised Units deal with corruption-related crimes:

- The Transparency and Anti-corruption Unit (Unidad de Transparencia y Lucha contra la Corrupción), which leads criminal investigation of acts of corruption and those that undermine transparency in public life.

- The Public Administration Unit (Unidad de Administración Pública), which investigates crimes of embezzlement, bribery, illicit enrichment and extortion.

Electoral branch

Lastly, the Electoral branch (*Función Electoral*) has crucial responsibilities in relation to the transparency and integrity of election processes and political financing. Firstly, the National Electoral Council (*Consejo Nacional Electoral*), whose functions include organising, directing, overseeing and guaranteeing the transparency of the electoral processes; controlling the electoral propaganda and expenditure, including budgets submitted by political organisations and candidates; guaranteeing the transparency and legality of the internal electoral processes of political organisations. Appeals against the acts of the National Electoral Council are decided by the Electoral Disputes Tribunal (*Tribunal Contencioso Electoral*), which can also impose sanctions for non-compliance with regulations on financing, propaganda, electoral expenditure and, in general, for violations of electoral regulations.

Current institutional arrangements do not enable effective co-operation among institutions with responsibilities for integrity policies at the national level and across State levels

To ensure that the various actors that are part of an integrity system work towards shared goals, taking advantage of synergies and avoiding gaps or overlaps, it is essential to establish co-operation among them. This is the case both among actors at the central level, but also between levels of government. In this sense, the *OECD Recommendation on Public Integrity* calls countries to "promote mechanisms for horizontal and vertical co-operation between such public officials, units or bodies and where possible, with and between sub-national levels of government, through formal or informal means to support coherence and avoid overlap and gaps, and to share and build on lessons learned from good practices" (OECD, 2017[6]).

While some co-operation mechanisms related to integrity matters have been put in place in relation to enforcement or between institutions within the same branch of the state, Ecuador does not have either formal or informal institutional arrangements on public integrity bringing together relevant actors belonging to all the State's branches in a comprehensive and systemic way.

Cross-branches initiatives

Co-ordination initiatives have been attempted in the past, but they did not manage to institutionalise themselves. The Anti-corruption Inter-institutional Roundtable (*Mesa interinstitucional para combatir la corrupción*), promoted by the President of the Republic in 2018, gathered representatives from all state's branches but it did not lead to any specific initiatives. Earlier on, the Front for Transparency and the Fight against Corruption (*Frente de Transparencia y Lucha contra la Corrupción*), consisting of representatives from the executive branch and civil society, was established by Executive Decree No. 21 of June 5, 2017, to propose the President strategies and mechanisms for the prevention of corruption in the public and private sector, as well as policies and regulations for transparency and the fight against corruption. The Front produced a report with recommendations, and among those, it was stressed the need to strengthen co-ordination mechanisms through the creation of a National System of Co-ordination and Control (Box 2.1), However, these recommendations did not lead to any normative or institutional reforms, including with regards to the development of comprehensive and permanent co-ordination mechanisms.

> ### Box 2.1. Proposed co-ordination arrangements by the Front for Transparency and the Fight against Corruption
>
> The final report produced by the Front for Transparency and the Fight against Corruption noted that several of the institutional and implementation challenges in the fight against corruption could be addressed by strengthening co-ordination mechanisms, which emerged as one of the priorities. In that sense, it also proposed the constitution of a National Control System, bringing together all relevant institutions and consisting of two co-ordination groups, one related to prevention and one to enforcement.
>
> In relation to the co-ordination needed on prevention, the Front stressed that the objective should be to harmonise regulations, to clarify competencies, to develop and improve control tools, to unify information, to enhance sectoral controls and to establish indicators and standards for managing and evaluating progress, as well as to focus on strategic sectors such as oil and mining activities.
>
> Source: Front for Transparency and the Fight against Corruption (2017[14]), *Proposals*, https://www.cenae.org/uploads/8/2/7/0/82706952/versio%CC%81n_final_151017_propuestas_finales_ftlc.pdf (accessed on 12 April 2021).

Enforcement-related initiatives

With regards to enforcement, an Inter-Institutional Co-operation Agreement to strengthen the fight against corruption and asset recovery was signed in 2019 by the heads of the Judicial Council (*Consejo de la Judicatura*), the Anti-corruption Secretariat (*Secretaría Anticorrupción*), the Comptroller General Office (*Contraloría General del Estado*), the Office of the Prosecutor General (*Fiscalía General del Estado*), the Office of the Attorney General (*Procuraduría General del Estado*) and the Financial Analysis Unit (*Unidad de Análisis Financiero*, UAFE). This agreement established several inter-institutional co-operation mechanisms, including the exchange of information, the collaboration in investigations and recovery of assets, the development of joint research and innovation projects as well as the implementation of professional training programmes. As part of this agreement, in January 2021, an "Inter-Institutional Roundtable for the Fight against Corruption" (*Mesa Interinstitucional de Lucha contra la Corrupción*) was created by the Judicial Council together with the National Court of Justice (*Corte Nacional de Justicia*), the Office of the Public Defender (*Defensoría Pública*), the Ministry of Government (*Ministerio de Gobierno*), the police and the Financial Analysis Unit . The objective of the roundtable is to implement inter-institutional co-operation mechanisms enabling the co-ordination of actions that address critical bottleneck and structural problems in the exercise of the criminal action. Plus, the roundtable is intended to facilitate the analysis of specific cases and the establishment of suitable protocols for the correct development of the justice service. The Inter-institutional Anti-Corruption Roundtable will meet regularly once a month and extraordinarily when the situation warrants it, and will establish deadlines, processes, a work schedule and periodic follow-up of the results.

Another operational mechanism for co-ordination has been set up in 2019 to facilitate and obtaining timely and effective results in asset recovery processes through the establishment of the Asset Recovery Inter-Agency Liaison Group (*Grupo de Enlaces Interinstitucionales para la Recuperación de Activos*, GEIRA), which is composed of 11 institutions: the Office of the Prosecutor General, the Office of the Attorney General, the Citizen Participation Council, the Financial Analysis Unit, the Ministry of Foreign Affairs and Human Mobility (*Ministerio de Relaciones Exteriores y Movilidad Humana*), the Anti-Corruption Secretariat, the Internal Revenue Service (*Servicio de Rentas Internas*), the Public Real Estate Secretariat (Inmobiliar), the Strategic Intelligence Centre (*Centro de Inteligencia Estratégica*), the National Court of Justice and the Judicial Council.

Co-ordination mechanisms within state's branches

As for co-ordination mechanisms internal to the state's branches, the Transparency and Social Control branch counts with a co-ordinating body, the Co-ordination Committee, composed by the head of each of the entities that comprise it, who each year elect the president of the branch from among its members. This committee has the responsibility, among others, to formulate public policies on transparency, social control, accountability, promotion of citizen participation, prevention and fight against corruption; co-ordinating the branch's entities action plans and the formulation of the National Plan for the Prevention and Fight against Corruption; presenting to the National Assembly proposals for legal reforms within the scope of its competence. In turn, the implementation and operationalisation of the work, policies and plan of the Co-ordination Committee are carried out by the Technical Secretariat, whose Secretary is appointed by the Committee out of three candidates proposed by the president. While formally these institutional arrangements could promote co-ordination within the Transparency and Social Control branch, the information provided highlighted that the capacity of the Technical Secretariat is *de facto* extremely limited because of the number of staff working in it, amounting to three public officials next to the Secretary.

Within the Executive, the Anti-corruption Secretariat dissolved by Executive Decree No. 1065 of May 21, 2020, was meant to mainstreaming the fight against corruption within the Executive branch. While the General Secretariat of the Presidency of the Republic has been transferred the documents and archives and has been promoting integrity initiatives as part of its work on open government, the former mandate and competences of the Anti-corruption Secretariat have not been formally transferred to any institution. In fact, the focus of the Anti-corruption Secretariat's activity was not on prevention but rather on the investigation of possible corruption cases (PADF; FCD; CSIS, 2020[15]) and this focus on investigations seems to have been one of the key reason that eventually led to its dissolution (El Comercio, 2020[16]). As a consequence, there is currently no co-ordinating entity on integrity and corruption prevention issues within the Executive, leading to a substantial institutional gap. This situation poses challenges to promote, co-ordinate and implement policies not only within public institutions and entities of the Executive (e.g. ministries, secretaries and state-owned enterprises), but also to co-ordinate actions with other state branches and society more broadly.

Co-ordination between the central and subnational entities

The lack of comprehensive co-operation mechanisms does not only concern the state's branches but also the different sub-national levels of the public administration, which are the Decentralised Autonomous Governments (provinces, cantons, and rural parishes). Some meaningful initiatives had been taken in the past, but they were either bilateral or they did not involve all relevant bodies and branches.

The Government of the Municipality of the Metropolitan District of Quito – through its integrity body *Quito Honesto* – had signed an agreement with the Anti-Corruption Secretariat created on February 6, 2019, to co-ordinate integrity and anti-corruption policies, but eventually this could not have been fully implemented because of the dissolution of the latter with Executive Decree No. 1065 of May 21, 2020.

The Council for Citizen Participation and Social Control developed the Model for Transparent and Participatory Territories (*Modelo de Territorios Transparentes y Participativos*), which defined action plans, products, tools and instruments to be implemented by GADs based on their context and reality in six components:

- training and continuous capacity building
- access to public information
- human development
- citizen participation and social control
- accountability
- institutional co-ordination (Council for Citizen Participation and Social Control of Ecuador, 2016[17]).

Similarly, no comprehensive initiatives have been taken to promote information exchanges or mutual learning between bodies with integrity or anti-corruption mandate within the GADs, neither by institutions at the state level nor by local co-ordination bodies such as the Consortium of provincial autonomous governments (*Consorcio de Gobiernos Autónomos Provinciales del Ecuador*, CONGOPE), the Association of Ecuadorian Municipalities (*Asociación de Minicipalidades Ecuatorianas*, AME) and the National Council of Rural Parish Governments of Ecuador (*Consejo Nacional de Gobiernos Parroquiales Rurales del Ecuador*, CONAGOPARE).

Ecuador could establish a National Integrity and Anti-corruption System to promote strategic co-operation and dialogue among the five state branches, between levels of administration and with the contribution of civil society, academia and private sector

According to the OECD experience, countries have been adopting various mechanisms to ensure co-operation on public integrity:

- Formal mechanisms to ensure coherent decision making and enable support, communication and information sharing.
- Informal mechanisms to enable horizontal exchange and support.
- Mechanisms tailored to national and sub-national levels in line with the country's governance framework (OECD, 2020[12]).

While there is no single model to address the co-operation challenges, some lessons which have been observed in the OECD work with countries in Latin America (Table 2.3) are relevant for the Ecuadorian context, namely:

- It is essential to create spaces for dialogue, reflection and co-operation between the branches and autonomous bodies which, while respecting their autonomy, enable taking advantage of common efforts to implement coherent public integrity agendas in all public domains, with a view to increasing its credibility and trust. While entities outside the executive branch often have the autonomy to implement their own integrity policies, it is vital to seek co-operation mechanisms that allow for the transfer of knowledge and support for their implementation. Some countries have multi-stakeholder co-ordination bodies, in which executive or control entities usually participate although their membership varies. In other cases, as in Colombia, Mexico and Peru, representatives of the judiciary participate as well. Only the co-ordination bodies in Colombia and Peru also include the participation of the legislative branch.
- For formal mechanisms to work, the following elements are necessary:
  - Leadership (will): particularly from the highest authority within the mechanism.
  - Management: they should set visible tasks, commitments and targets leading to high impact products and have operational or implementing units that are responsible for implementing and following up on the commitments that emerge.
  - Capacity: Implementing units need authority to guide and follow up co-ordination, this may include, for example, drafting legislation and policies, leading the development of a National Integrity and Anti-Corruption Strategy, and/or monitoring and evaluating integrity policies.
- It may be difficult to have a single co-ordination mechanism, or to include all relevant actors in it. This could be solved by establishing alternate, but integrated co-ordination spaces that feed into a core group (inter-institutional working groups or commissions with rotating leadership, for example).
- Although in most of the experiences there is no direct participation of civil society in the co-ordinating units, there is a growing trend to increase the formal involvement of civil society and

the participation of non-governmental actors in the integrity system. For example, in Colombia and Mexico there are particular mechanisms for including civil society representation. On the one hand, in Colombia, the 2011 Anti-Corruption Statute created the National Citizen Commission for the Fight against Corruption (*Comisión Nacional Ciudadana para la Lucha Contra la Corrupción*, CNCLCC), which is the body representing Colombian citizens to evaluate and improve policies that promote ethical conduct and curb corruption in the public and private sectors. On the other hand, in Mexico, the National Anti-Corruption System (*Sistema Nacional Anticorrupción*) established in 2015 has among its governing bodies a Citizen Participation Committee (*Comites de participación Ciudadana*), which aims to be the body that links with social and academic organisations related to the matters of the National System. In Peru, the co-ordinating body on integrity and anti-corruption issues, the High-level Commission against Corruption (*Comisión de Alto Nivel Anticorrupción*, CAN), is also made up of non-governmental actors, including representatives of private business entities, trade union organisations, universities, the media and religious institutions (OECD, 2019[1]).

Table 2.3. Public integrity systems in the LAC region

Country	Integrity Policy Co-ordinating Agency	Horizontal Co-ordination	Participation of the legislative branch	Participation of the Judicial branch	Other actors participation
Argentina	Secretary of Institutional Strengthening (*Secretaría de Fortalecimiento Institucional*) in the Executive Office of the Cabinet of Ministers	Informal through work tables System is in the process of being reformed	No	No	No
Colombia	Secretary of Transparency (*Secretaría de Transparencia*, ST)	National Moralization Commission (CNM)	Si	Si	National Citizens' Committee for the Fight against Corruption
Chile	Ministry of the General Secretariat of the Presidency (*Ministerio Secretaría General de la Presidencia*)	Probity and Transparency Commission	No	No	An anti-corruption alliance was established as a working group with the private sector and civil society, but they do not participate in the co-ordination structure.
Costa Rica	n.a.	Informal, by agreement between the institutions	n.a.	n.a.	n.a.
Mexico	Executive Secretary of the National Anti-corruption System *Secretaría Ejecutiva del Sistema Nacional Anticorrupción*)	Co-ordinating committee of the National Anti-corruption System	No	Si	Citizen participation committee
Peru	Secretary of Public Integrity (*Secretaría de Integridad Pública*) in the Presidency of the Council of Ministers	High-level anti-corruption commission	Si	Si	Includes private sector, trade unions, medium universities and religious institutions (with voice but no vote)

Source: OECD (2019[1]), *La Integridad Pública en América Latina y el Caribe 2018-2019*, OECD, Paris, http://www.oecd.org/gov/integridad/integridad-publica-en-america-latina-caribe-2018-2019.htm (accessed on 25 february 2020).

Considering the institutional set-up of the country and the lessons learnt from countries in the LAC region, Ecuador could consider establishing a National Integrity and Anti-corruption System to address the weak co-operation among all actors with a public integrity and anti-corruption mandate. This system should bring together relevant institutions from all branches of the State and levels of the public administration and have the key mission to ensure continuous dialogue and define co-operation initiatives with due consideration of the role and responsibilities assigned to each of them by the Constitution. Such a system would be coherent with a similar proposal made by an expert group in the past (Box 2.1) and would make use of a model of co-operation which is successfully used in other policy areas such as violence against women and public procurement (Box 2.2).

Box 2.2. The National Gender and Public Procurement Systems in Ecuador

The **Comprehensive National System to Prevent and Eradicate Violence against Women** (*Sistema Nacional Integral para Prevenir y Erradicar la Violencia contra las Mujeres*) is defined as the organised and co-ordinated group of institutions, norms, policies, plans, programmes, mechanisms and activities aimed at preventing and eradicating violence against women, through prevention, care, protection and comprehensive reparation of the rights of victims.

The law establishing the system defines its scope, which is to prevent and eradicate violence against women through the design, formulation, execution, supervision, monitoring and evaluation of norms, policies, programmes, mechanisms and actions, in all instances and at all levels of government, in an articulated and co-ordinated manner. Furthermore, it defines the governing body, which is the Secretariat of Human Rights. The following members have the obligation to articulate and co-ordinate among themselves and with other relevant actors all related actions:

- Governing Body for Justice and Human Rights
- Governing body for Education
- Governing Body for Higher Education
- Governing Body for Health
- Governing Body for Public Security and Public Order
- Governing Body for Labour
- Governing Body for Economic and Social Inclusion
- National Equality Councils
- Council for Regulation and Development of Information and Communication;
- National Institute of Statistics and Census
- Integrated Security Service ECU 911
- Judicial Council
- Office of the Attorney General
- Office of the Public Defender
- Office of the Ombudsman
- One representative elected by the assembly of each associative body of the Decentralised Autonomous Governments.

The Organic Law of the **National Public Procurement System** (*Ley Orgánica del Sistema Nacional de Contratación Pública*) establishes that the National Public Procurement Service (*Servicio Nacional de Contratación Pública*) is the governing body of the National Public Procurement System (*Sistema Nacional de Contratación*).

The Board of the National Public Procurement Service – which is responsible for planning, prioritising, proposing and issuing the national public procurement policy, establishing the public procurement sector rules or policies for public entities; and adopting the regulations for the organisation and operation of the National Public Procurement Service – consists of:

- The Minister responsible for Production, Employment and Competitiveness
- The highest authority of the National Planning Agency
- The Minister of Finance
- The Mayor appointed by the General Assembly of the Association of Municipalities of Ecuador
- The Prefect appointed by the Consortium of Provincial Councils of Ecuador
- The highest authority of the body responsible for economic inclusion
- The General Director of the National Public Procurement Service, who acts as Secretary of the Board of Directors but cannot express vote.

Source: (National Assembly of Ecuador, 2018[18]); (National Assembly of Ecuador, 2008[19]).

Ecuador could take the opportunity to include the development of such a National Integrity and Anti-corruption System as one of the priority objectives on public integrity of the National Development Plan 2021-2025, which could also set the foundations on which to build a strategic approach and vision for public integrity. Learning from past attempts to establish co-operation mechanisms but also considering the experience collected during the fact-finding mission, this National Integrity and Anti-corruption System should build on a dialogue phase among all relevant actors, which would ensure legitimacy of the process as well as ownership and commitment of all institutions. This dialogue should also include spaces for civil society and the private sector to share ideas, inputs and priorities in shaping the system. As highlighted by interviews during the fact-finding mission, it is also important that the National Integrity and Anti-corruption System is established in a law – rather than an executive decree – and explicitly mentions the duty to co-operate of each participating institution in order to ensure compliance and the sustainability of the system.

With regards to the governance of the National Integrity and Anti-corruption System, it is recommended that the President of the Republic, as head of the State, (Figure 2.1) leads and presides it. This would show the highest level of commitment to integrity and anti-corruption issues and ensure proactive institutional co-operation among all five branches of the State, while respecting their constitutional roles and functions. Such institutional arrangement would also take into account the OECD experience, as often the co-ordinating role of such formalised arrangements requires the highest degree of influence, authority and leadership and is located at a visible and central place to signal its importance, such as in the president's office, or under the council of ministers. Next to the President, this system should include all relevant institutions from the five State branches, as well as representatives from Regional Decentralised Authorities in order to ensure coherency and leverage synergies between respective policies and initiatives (Box 2.3).

> ### Box 2.3. Examples of integrity and anti-corruption policies and initiatives in the legislative and judicial branch, as well as in the Municipality of the Metropolitan District of Quito
>
> The **National Assembly of Ecuador** (NA) has set a website (www.asambleanacional.gob.ec/es/leyes-aprobadas) to strengthen legislative transparency and oversight of processes carried out by the NA, which is one of the objectives of its Institutional Strategic Plan 2019 - 2021. The National Assembly is also implementing an Anti-Bribery Management System based on the 37001 standard of the International Organization for Standardization (ISO) and as part of this process it has adopted an Integrity Manual that defines a strategy based on the promotion of integrity and transparency aiming at improving management and institutional reputation. In August 2019, the Legislative Administration Council (*Consejo de Administración Legislativa*), through Resolution CAL-2019-2021-083, amended the Organic Functional Regulations of the National Assembly of Ecuador to create the General Co-ordination of Integrity and Prevention.
>
> The **Judicial Council**, through its Judicial Service School, has developed and disseminated educational tools for justice operators with the aim of strengthening judicial integrity and preventing corruption in the judicial system, in accordance with the requirements of article 11 of the UNCAC and the Bangalore Principles of Judicial Conduct. To further implement these commitments, it joined the Global Judicial Integrity Network on 14 May 2020.
>
> The **Municipality of the Metropolitan District of Quito** (MDMQ) is working on an anti-corruption plan, through the metropolitan Commission for the Fight against Corruption (*Quito Honesto*), an entity in charge, according to its competences, of preventing, controlling and investigating possible acts of corruption. Furthermore, examples of initiatives that have been developed as mechanisms to mitigate corruption are:
>
> - Training and Education Plan developed jointly with the Municipal Training Institute (ICAM) aiming to ensure understanding of the responsibilities and ethical rules governing the activities of municipal public officials as well as strengthening values and principles to promote an institutional ethical culture in the fulfilment of their functions.
> - Review of control mechanisms and strategies adopted by municipal entities, which are classified according to the products and services they deliver.
> - Creation of a link in all portals of the MDMQ so that citizens can file complaints about possible cases of corruption within municipal entities.
>
> Source: Answers to OECD questionnaire; (UNDOC, 2020[20]).

The law creating the National Integrity and Anti-corruption System should identify roles and a set of functions which are coherent with the constitutional mandates and the priorities, as discussed and defined during the dialogue phase. Considering the previously-identified weaknesses, it should as a minimum:

- Ensure the participation and contribution of all actors in the design of the National Integrity and Anti-corruption Strategy as well as of national integrity and anti-corruption policies.
- Co-ordinate the implementation of integrity and anti-corruption policies, and in particular the National Integrity and Anti-corruption Strategy.
- Monitor and communicate activities of all actors which are part of the System and their progress in the implementation of integrity and anti-corruption policies, in particular of the National Integrity and Anti-corruption Strategy.
- Develop studies building on data and knowledge of various institutions to identify fraud and corruption risk areas, trends, priorities for possible co-ordinated action.

- Generate communication and awareness campaigns about public integrity and the National Integrity and Anti-corruption System.
- Stimulate co-operation and the exchange of good practices.

As for the operational functioning, the System should gather the heads of the participating institutions in annual plenary meetings to report on the activities, while close advisors of the head of the institution should be appointed to co-ordinate the work at more technical level.

Civil society organisations should not only be part of the dialogue phase leading up to the National Integrity and Anti-corruption System, but also participate in the system itself, at least with the possibility to be invited to meetings, to bring proposals, and to monitor the activities of the system. For this purpose, Ecuador could benefit from the input of the organisations that have participated in the development of the open government plan (Box 2.5) as well as other co-ordination initiatives from civil society and the private sector (Table 2.4).

Table 2.4. Co-ordinated initiatives from civil society and private sector

Actor	Mandate and functions
National Anti-corruption Commission (*Comisión Nacional Anticorrupción*)	Civil society body created in 2015 by mandate of the National Collective of Workers, Indigenous Peoples and Social Organizations of Ecuador. The Commission proposed four questions for the popular referendum of 2018, including one related to the Council of Citizen Participation and Social Control. In addition, it has filed several complaints with the Office of the Prosecutor General for irregularities in contracts of different public institutions.
Integrity and Anti-corruption Commission (*Comisión de Integridad y Anticorrupción*)	With the support of the International Chamber of Commerce - Ecuador Chapter (ICC), the Integrity and Anti-corruption Commission was formed in 2019. 27 members form it: one president, two vice-presidents, and 24 additional members, including representatives of the private sector, members of the Academy and civil society organisations. Its objective is to promote the integrity and fight against corruption in companies and public sector entities, promote the adoption of anti-corruption policies in the business sector and the use of ICC rules and tools to combat corruption, including the Agreement for Ethics and Transparency.
Ecuador's Citizen Innovation laboratory (*Laboratorio de Innovación Ciudadana*)	As part of its Open Government Plan, Ecuador is working on the implementation of the first citizen innovation laboratory to generate spaces contributing to public management's improvement through the co-creation and collaboration of citizens. In particular, the Laboratory aims to: • improve public service • co-create innovative solutions to address social issues, especially those related to vulnerable populations • modernise the relationship between governmental and non-governmental actors • generate new channels for citizen inputs.

Building a vision on integrity and anti-corruption in Ecuador

Ecuador could embrace a strategic approach to public integrity

A public integrity strategy is essential for supporting and sustaining a coherent and comprehensive integrity system as well as the actions of the institutions that form part of it. This does not only include the document itself, but also the process for its development, which is perhaps as important as the resulting strategy. Thanks to an inclusive and participative process and a solid evidence base, a strategy can be legitimised, identify the most impactful risks and agree on meaningful strategic objectives for the country. Strategies are also a way of demonstrating commitment but can also erode trust and credibility of public authorities if they do not lead to actions or their progress is not subject to monitoring and evaluation (OECD, 2020[12]). In line with this approach, the *OECD Recommendation on Public Integrity* states that adherents should "develop a strategic approach for the public sector that is based on evidence and aimed at mitigating public integrity risks, in particular through:

- Setting strategic objectives and priorities for the public integrity system based on a risk-based approach to violations of public integrity standards, taking into account factors that contribute to effective public integrity policies.
- Developing benchmarks and indicators and gathering credible and relevant data on the level of implementation, performance and overall effectiveness of the public integrity system" (OECD, 2017[6]).

While Ecuador does have some strategic objectives defined in the National Development Plan 2017-2021 and the National Public Integrity and Anti-corruption Plan 2019-2023, both planning instruments have not been able to generate the expected impact.

The National Development Plan 2017-2021

Ecuador has declared the fight against corruption a national priority and included integrity-related objectives in its National Development Plan for 2017-2021 *"Toda una Vida"* (*Plan Nacional de Desarrollo 2017 – 2021 Toda una Vida*). However, this has not generated visible results. The National Plan for Good Living 2017-2021 (*Plan Nacional para el Buen Vivir 2017 – 2021*) established six actions aimed at strengthening transparency and the fight against corruption in the public and private sectors, as part of objective no. 8 on "Promoting transparency and co-responsibility for a new social ethic" (*Promover la transparencia y la corresponsabilidad para una nueva ética social*) that was developed also based on the proposals of the Front for Transparency and the Fight against Corruption:

- Promote a new social ethic, based on solidarity, co-responsibility, equity and social justice, as principles and values that guide the behaviour and actions of society and its various sectors.
- Strengthen the transparency of public policies and the fight against corruption, with better access to high-quality public information, optimising the accountability policies and promoting participation and social control.
- Promote measures for the prevention of conflicts of interest and opacity in State contracts.
- Combat impunity by strengthening inter-institutional co-ordination and the effectiveness of processes for the detection, investigation, trial, sanction and execution of sentences.
- Promote an international ethical pact to achieve tax justice, the elimination of tax havens, and the fight against tax evasion and avoidance.
- Strengthen transparency in the private and popular sector, promoting the adoption of integrity tools that strengthen the principles of co-operativism and corporate governance, discouraging the commission of acts that undermine national development objectives.

To support the implementation and the monitoring of the Plan, a Strategic Cabinet (*Gabinete Estratégico*) and four Sectoral Cabinets (*Gabinetes Sectoriales*), were established. However, information available online and collected in the interviews manifested the lack of any continuous monitoring of the Plan, raising concerns over the rate of implementation and the results achieved by public entities in relation to those objectives, which touched upon some key issues as inter-institutional co-ordination and conflict of interest.

The National Public Integrity and Anti-corruption Plan 2019-2023

The Transparency and Social Control branch developed and adopted the National Public Integrity and Anti-corruption Plan for 2019-2023 (*Plan Nacional de Integridad Pública y Lucha contra la Corrupción 2019-2023*) (Transparency and Social Control Function of Ecuador, 2019[21]) based on the analysis of the national context as well as data on emblematic corruption cases and perception of corrupt practices among citizens. The Plan identifies key causes of corruption and actions to address them, aiming to achieve the following strategic objectives:

- promote integrity in the public and private management of public resources

- strengthen citizen action in all its organisational forms so that it generates impact in public life
- strengthen public and private inter-institutional co-ordination and co-operation mechanisms that develop preventive and anti-corruption initiatives and actions.

Each strategic objective has an indicator and consists of different strategies, which in turn correspond to a project, various activities and a set of responsible entities.

The Plan builds on an analytical framework, which includes reference to the OECD definition of public integrity (OECD, 2017[6]), and defines a matrix with objectives and goals as well as a list of projects, activities and responsible entities. However, the document and the interviews during the fact-finding mission evidenced that the involvement of public entities outside the Transparency and Social Control branch as well as of representatives from civil society was very limited in the development process.

Furthermore, the matrix makes only minor reference to entities from other branches, whereas many key actions such as the development of a Code of Conduct for the public sector and of risk management mechanisms to prevent corruption and unethical conduct, the implementation of a training programme for public officials and education curricula for students, as well as the strengthening of inter-institutional co-ordination mechanisms cannot be fully implemented without the involvement and co-responsibility of other public entities, especially from the Executive branch (e.g. Presidency of the Republic, Ministry of Labour, and Ministry of Education). The inward-looking perspective of the Plan may explain the limited advancement in its implementation, which interviewees also attributed to the difficulties caused by the COVID-19 pandemic and to the limited resources and capacity of the body in charge of promoting and co-ordinating its implementation, which is the Technical Secretariat of the Transparency and Social Control branch's Co-ordination Committee. Furthermore, interviewees pointed out the lack of continuous engagement and commitment among the members of the Transparency and Social Control branch itself. Regardless of the specific causes, the Plan demonstrated to have had very limited impact so far and most actors from the public sector, civil society and private sector interviewed during the fact-finding mission had little or no awareness of the existence of the Plan and of its actions.

The National Development Plan 2021-2025 could set the roadmap for the progressive and participative development of a National Integrity and Anti-corruption Strategy

Although efforts have been made to define integrity-related objectives and activities, they do not provide relevant institutions and the public with a clear and evidence-based strategy addressing risk areas and priorities. As a result, representatives from various institutions interviewed during the fact-finding mission indicated the lack of a national "vision" on integrity and anti-corruption matters as one of the most significant challenges of the country. Indeed, this is considered one of the main causes of the fragmented and incoherent initiatives of the last year, which in turn contributed to the low levels of public confidence in the anti-corruption efforts and government action more broadly.

This challenge is closely linked with the weakness related to co-operation, which is a pre-requisite in so far as a strategy needs the contribution and participation of all relevant entities across different branches, whose acceptance and active engagement is critical for the strategy to succeed. At the same time, the implementation process of a strategy can also further reinforce and promote co-operation and synergies when it comes to assigning the shared responsibility to implement objectives to two or more relevant actors, or to an actor in close co-ordination with other ones.

Ecuador should take advantage of the National Development Plan 2021-2025 not only to set the creation of a National Integrity and Anti-corruption System as an objective, but also to define a roadmap with progressive steps and objectives aiming and leading towards a National Integrity and Anti-corruption Strategy. While reflecting the priorities of the President of the Republic in relation to public integrity, such a strategy should aim at going beyond the government in turn and contribute to build a vision for the country (Figure 2.2).

Figure 2.2. Integrity-related objectives for the National Development Plan 2021-2025

Source: Elaborated by the OECD based on the recommendations.

Including this objective on the National Integrity and Anti-corruption Strategy - as well as the one creating the National Integrity and Anti-corruption System - into the National Development Plan has various key advantages. First, the National Development Plan has the highest constitutional legitimacy and status since national development planning is one of the essential constitutional duties of the State (Article 3 of the Constitution) and because Article 280 of the Constitution establishes that it is the strategic document that informs:

- public policies, programmes and projects, including the integrity and anti-corruption ones
- the programming and execution of the State budget
- and the investment and allocation of public resources (Box 2.4).

Second, the National Development Plan is approved and monitored by the National Planning Council (*Consejo Nacional de Planificación*), which is a broad participative mechanism presided by the President of the Republic and including representatives from subnational levels of government. The work of the National Planning Council, including the development of the National Development Plan is supported by the Technical Secretariat "Planifica Ecuador" (*Secretaría Técnica Planifica Ecuador*), an entity part of the Presidency of the Republic which succeeded to an independent, Ministry-level entity, the National Secretariat for Planning and Development (*Secretaría Nacional de Planificación y Desarrollo*, SENPLADES), following Executive Decree No. 732 of May 13, 2019.

Third, the observance of the National Development Plan is mandatory for all institutions in the public sector, which would also promote and ensure the engagement of all branches of the State.

Box 2.4. The National Development Plan in Ecuador

The decentralised national participatory planning system organises development planning. The system is made up of a National Planning Council, which integrates the different levels of government, with citizen participation, and has a technical secretariat, which co-ordinates it. This council has the objective of dictating the guidelines and policies that orient the system and approving the National Development Plan, and is presided over by the President of the Republic.

The National Development Plan connects short and medium-term public policies with a long-term vision in line with the Constitution. The Plan informs any public action, programme and project, the public budget and debts, international co-operation, state-owned enterprises and social security. At the same time, plans of decentralised autonomous governments should also be defined in the framework of the National Development Plan. This shall also incorporate the long-term national public policy policies that have been established through popular consultation.

The National Development Plan is approved by the National Planning Council, which is the body in charge of the decentralised national participatory planning system (*Sistema nacional descentralizado de planificación participativa*). Such Council is presided by the President of the Republic, has a technical secretariat (Technical Secretariat "Planifica Ecuador", *Secretaría Técnica Planifica Ecuador*), includes all levels of government and provides for citizens' participation mechanisms.

The National Development Plan lasts for a period of four years based on the government programme of the President-elect, and in consideration of the general objectives of the plans of the other functions of the State and the development plans of the Decentralised Autonomous Governments, within the scope of their competencies. The development of the Plan must ensure citizens participation.

Source: National Assembly of Ecuador (2010[22]), Planning and Public Finance Organic Code, https://www.gob.ec/sites/default/files/regulations/2020-06/C%C3%93DIGO_ORG%C3%81NICO_DE_PLANIFICACI%C3%93N_Y_FINANZAS%20-%20diciembre%202019.pdf (accessed on 12 April 2021).

In view of taking advantage of already existing initiatives taken by Ecuador and considering the 4-year validity of the National Development Plan, the roadmap to be laid down could aim at developing a National Integrity and Anti-corruption Strategy in two sequenced steps (Figure 2.3):

- As the first step, starting in 2022 and following the creation of the National Integrity and Anti-corruption System recommended above, the National Development Plan could give the mandate to this System to co-ordinate the development of an Action Plan to implement some key priority actions of the National Public Integrity and Anti-corruption Plan 2019-2023 adopted by the Transparency and Social Control Function. In spite of the limited results and involvement of relevant actors, the National Public Integrity and Anti-corruption Plan 2019-2023 identifies some areas of intervention where weakness have also been identified by the present report, such as on code of ethics, risk-management, training. Plus, using the existing plan would send a positive message to citizens, civil society and the private sector showing an effort to ensure the continuity of integrity and anti-corruption policies. However, the Action Plan should focus on a set of priorities, rely on the support of National Integrity and Anti-corruption System to ensure a broader involvement of all branches of the State in its design and implementation, as well as receive feedback and comments from civil society. Such an action plan should focus on addressing high-risk areas, realistic objectives, and also achieving some visible results to regain trust of the public. In this sense, the OECD experience suggests laying emphasis on the communication of the action plan, which should be kept simple and enable readers from outside the public administration to understand actions, responsibilities and expected results.

- As a second step, starting in 2022, the National Development Plan could envisage the development of a new National Public Integrity and Anti-corruption Strategy for the 2023-2026 term, making it a state strategy going beyond the term of the government mandate (2021-2025) and thus contributing to building continuity over political changes. In turn, the Strategy could be implemented through two Action Plans covering a two-year period each (2023-2024; 2025-2026). Based on the experience of OECD countries, the National Public Integrity and Anti-corruption Strategy could consider the following methodological steps of the process:
  - o Problem analysis: risk identification, analysis and mitigation.
  - o Strategy design: prioritising the objectives, policy consultation and co-ordination.
  - o Development of indicators with baselines, milestones and targets.
  - o Drafting of the action plan, distributing responsibilities and costing activities.
  - o Implementation, monitoring, evaluation, and communication of the results of monitoring and evaluation, including evaluation prior to implementation (OECD, 2020[12]):

Among the inputs to consider throughout this process, the Strategy and Action Plans could also build on the analysis and recommendations from a potential OECD Integrity Review of Ecuador.

Figure 2.3. Sequencing of the recommended measures to create a National Integrity and Anti-corruption System and to develop a National Integrity and Anti-corruption Strategy

Source: Elaborated by the OECD based on the recommendations.

Given the multiplicity of institutions with integrity-related responsibilities in Ecuador, the development process of this National Public Integrity and Anti-corruption Strategy should be supported by adequate institutional arrangements to ensure co-ordination, participation and contribution of all relevant actors in its design and implementation. For this purpose, Ecuador would ideally assign the co-ordination of this process to the National Integrity and Anti-corruption System as recommended above. This would be in line with the practice of some OECD countries that delegated the responsibility for developing a strategy to a small committee composed of representatives from key relevant bodies in each branch of the State and from subnational entities. This drafting committee is ideally chaired by an individual with recognised stature, expertise, legitimacy and political influence to act as an effective "champion" for the drafting body, and ultimately for the strategy itself (UNODC, 2015[23]). For example, the UK Anti-corruption Strategy was drafted by the Joint Anti-Corruption Unit (JACU) in the Home Office, and the anti-corruption strategy in Finland was developed by a cross-government group that included police, local government and CSOs (Pyman, Eastwood and Elliott, 2017[24]).

To ensure the quality of the Strategy and Action Plans, Ecuador could also consider building capacities amongst the members of the National Integrity and Anti-corruption System in relation to strategic and operational planning with the technical support and methodologies of the Technical Secretariat "Planifica Ecuador". This would help building a common understanding of the challenges, priorities and key elements of integrity and anti-corruption policies, following international conventions and standards, such as the *OECD Recommendation on Public Integrity*.

The involvement of organisations from civil society and the private sector, which in Ecuador are active on a wide range of integrity-related issues, should also be ensured since it would help increase the legitimacy of the strategy and be essential to build a common vision (UNODC, 2015[23]). Such a common understanding is very much needed according to the interviews conducted during the fact-finding mission. In this sense, Ecuador could ensure a participative and inclusive methodology taking inspiration from the co-creation methodology used for the first Open Government Action Plan which was considered a successfully inclusive practice by many actors interviewed during the fact-finding mission (Box 2.5), as well as from methodologies used in other countries in the LAC region to develop their integrity and anti-corruption strategies (Box 2.6). In line with the model proposed for the National Integrity and Anti-corruption System, civil society organisations, private sector, the media, academics and the public, in general, could also be involved in the monitoring and evaluation of the strategy (UNDP, 2014[25]). Furthermore, the document should also be discussed by the broader population through a public consultation process, making available to the public all supporting documentation and clarifying how comments provided by the public and organisations have been considered in the final version of the strategy, including explanations for those comments not taken on board.

Box 2.5. Co-creation methodology for Ecuador's first Open Government Action Plan 2019-2022

The process of co-creation of Ecuador's first Open Government Action Plan started with the establishment of the Core Group, which is the space designed for the co-ordination, support and monitoring of the results of the co-creation process and the implementation of the Open Government Action Plan. Such space aimed to promote participation and co-operation between various actors as well as debate, consensus, balance and a plurality of voices. The members of the Core Group - institutions and entities from the academia, civil society and public sector - were selected according to their background, responsibilities and experience, and hold regular meetings to promote open government actions in the country. From the side of the public sector, the General Secretariat of the Presidency of the Republic is the Ministerial contact point responsible for co-ordinating the Open Government Partnership's activities at the national level and one of the public sector actors that contributed to the co-creation of the country's Open Government Action Plan by being part of the Open Government Core Group.

The methodology for the development of the Open Government Action Plan was based on co-creation at all stages in consideration of the key role of participation and collaboration in the design and implementation of responses to fundamental problems of society. Based on that, no decision related to the Plan could be taken exclusively by a governmental authority or by any of the members of the Core Group.

The methodology of the co-creation model aimed to guarantee three levels of participation: the general public; the Open Government Working Group and the Core Group. Plus, the process benefitted from learning experiences from other countries such as Argentina, Uruguay and Costa Rica.

As for its steps, the methodology consisted of the following ones:

1. Reception of ideas and proposals from citizens, civil society organisations, academia, government, and the private sector through the official Open Government website of Ecuador as well as territorial co-creation roundtables.

2. Preliminary analysis and grouping of proposals.

3. Evaluation of proposals according to their feasibility and relevance.

4. Selection of proposals with the highest potential to be included in the Open Government Action Plan, both in terms of their feasibility of implementation and their relevance or impact for Ecuador.

5. Validation by the highest authorities of the represented entities to ensure the feasibility of the proposals' implementation. After validation and confirmation, they become commitments of the Action Plan.

6. Creating accountability through a follow-up report in Ecuador's Open Government website on the proposal's selection as well as through an online communication campaign.

7. Formal adoption of the Action Plan through public presentation in Ecuador and to the Open Government Partnership.

Source: Open Government Ecuador (2019[26]), *Open Government Action Plan of Ecuador 2019-2022*, https://www.opengovpartnership.org/wp-content/uploads/2020/01/Ecuador_Action-Plan_2019-2021.pdf (accessed on 12 April 2021).

Box 2.6. Participative practices for the development of integrity and anti-corruption plans, policies and strategies in LAC

Anti-corruption National Plan of Argentina 2019-2023

An open public consultation was promoted by the Anti-corruption Office, through the portal of the Secretariat of Government of Modernisation. As a result of this process, several proposals were received related to institutional strengthening, citizen participation, integrity in the private sector, and school education on ethics.

Anti-corruption National Policy of Mexico (2020)

The public consultation process consisted of three pillars. The first was an advisory council, which was conceived as a space for high-level dialogue, in which representatives of civil society organisations, academia, the private sector, public institutions and international organisations participated, contributing studies, reports and research that were considered for the development of the policy proposal. The second pillar was the online citizen consultation through 64 interviews with different actors asking ask citizens and specialists about their perceptions of the causes, effects and possible solutions to the problem of corruption. The third pillar of the citizen consultation was implemented through eight regional forums to gather opinions and proposals from academics, civil society organisations and public officials from the country's state entities. The information gathered in this phase of the consultation provided a regional and local perspective on the phenomenon of corruption.

National Integrity, Transparency and Antic-corruption Plan of Paraguay 2021-2025

A broad participatory process was carried out to gather ideas from a large and varied group of sectors and individuals linked to the public service (120 authorities and civil servants from 81 public institutions) regarding possible barriers and facilitators to implement the National Plan. This included nine workshops and consultations with representatives of different sectors of civil society. Three of the workshops were held with officials from the three branches of government, including officials from the Comptroller General's Office, the Office of the Prosecutor General, the Central Bank of Paraguay and Itaipú Binacional. Three other meetings were held with government officials from Municipalities and Departments, and the three more with officials in charge of the Transparency and Anti-Corruption Units (*Unidad de Transparencia y Anticorrupción,* UTA) of public institutions. In general, the results of the consultative process aligned with the previous findings and the challenges identified in existing studies on the degree of development of Paraguay's institutional integrity system show.

National Integrity and Anti-corruption Policy of Peru (2017)

The development of the "National Integrity and Anti-Corruption Policy" was performed through a participatory process carried out by the High Level Anti-Corruption Commission (*Comisión De Alto Nivel Anticorrupción,* CAN) through its General Co-ordination, through the systematisation, analysis, design and prioritisation of the comments, contributions and suggestions obtained from various public entities and the private sector.

This process included:

- A technical workshop that allowed for the analysis and discussion of the content of the future national policy.
- A discussion of the first draft of the national policy with the contact points of the public and private entities represented in the High Level Anti-Corruption Commission and the representatives of all the ministries of the Executive branch, also through a virtual platform in place for the CAN contact points.
- Reception and contribution from the National Assembly of Regional Governments (*Asamblea Nacional de Gobiernos Regionales*) and the Association of Municipalities of Peru (*Asociación de Municipalidades del Perú*).
- Technical advice provided by the National Centre for Strategic Planning (CEPLAN), the Co-ordination Secretariat (*Secretaria de Coordinación*) and the Public Management Secretariat (*Secretaría de Gestión Pública*), so that the content and structure aligned to the Strategic Plan for National Development (*Plan Estratégico de Desarrollo Nacional*).

Source: (Government of Argentina, 2019[27]); (Anti-corruption System of Mexico, 2020[28]); (Government of Paraguay, 2020[29]); (Government of Peru, 2017[30]).

After the adoption of the Integrity and Anti-corruption Strategy for the 2023-2026 term, Ecuador could discuss and develop a long-term Integrity and Anti-corruption state policy linked to the Constitution and the Sustainable Development Goals

The experience, processes, participative methodologies and strategic approach for developing the National Integrity and Anti-corruption Strategy for the 2023-2026 term could lay the basis for a further step to consolidate and institutionalise a national integrity and anti-corruption vision in Ecuador. Once the Integrity and Anti-corruption Strategy is adopted, Ecuador could consider the development of a long-term state policy (*"Política de largo plazo"*) on integrity and anti-corruption, which is a strategic planning tool provided for in its legal framework informing the priorities of all following National Development Plans (Technical Secretariat Planifica Ecuador, 2019[31]). This policy would allow to further address the challenges of institutionalisation, continuity and sustainability of integrity and anti-corruption policies, which have been raised as one of the priorities during the fact-finding interviews.

The Technical Standard of the National Decentralised System for Participative Planning (*Norma Tecnica del Sistema Nacional Descentralizado de Planificación Participativa*) defines these long-term policies as state policies established based on a broad national agreement and the development of a common project for the future, based on constitutional duties and long-term international commitments. Accordingly, the long-term Integrity and Anti-corruption state policy could use the participative methodology developed for the strategy and envision its ratification through a popular referendum, which would increase its democratic legitimacy and demonstrate the state's commitment and engagement. Content-wise, the policy should contribute to fulfil one of Ecuador's key constitutional duties, which is to guarantee its inhabitants the right to a culture of peace, to integral security and to live in a democratic society free of corruption (Article 3 of the Constitution of Ecuador). It would also contribute to the implementation of internal commitments such as the United Nations Convention against Corruption and the Sustainable Development Goal no. 16 on Peace, Justice and Strong Institutions which is part of the 2030 for Sustainable Agenda and includes the target to substantially reduce corruption and bribery in all their forms and to develop effective, accountable and transparent institutions at all levels. The legal framework defines the structure and process for the adoption of such a long-term policy and sets its validity for a period of at least 20 years (Box 2.7). In developing its long-term policy, Ecuador could consider the national policy adopted by Peru in 2017, which sets the integrity and anti-corruption vision of the country and informs its plans and efforts (Box 2.8).

Box 2.7. Responsibilities and structure of long-term state policies in Ecuador

The Technical Secretariat of the National Decentralised System of Participatory Planning (*Secretaría Técnica del Sistema Nacional Descentralizado de Planificación Participativa*) co-ordinates the development of the long-term policies proposals for their validation by the National Planning Council (*Consejo Nacional de planificación*). The process of formulation and/or updating of the long-term policies includes co-ordination with the entities of the State and civil society through citizen participation bodies.

The long-term policies shall contain at least:

- National Long-Term Development Goals: These are the national goals agreed upon in participatory processes that reflect the structural change desired to achieve development within the framework of a common project for the future. Given that future challenges are diverse, the identification of national development objectives necessarily implies a prioritisation exercise.

- Long-term National Goals: Establishes the quantitative levels to be achieved in a given period of time. They must contain expressions with terms associated with quantity and time and are constructed with impact indicators that show a change or discontinuity with respect to the initial situation. Long-term goals must contribute to the achievement of the National Development Goals and are the basis for monitoring and evaluation.

- Long-term Territorial Model: Territorial expression of the Long-term Policies and their long-term goals and targets. It contains territorial guidelines that are orientations for the application of long-term policies in the territory.

Source: Technical Secretariat Planifica Ecuador (2019[31]), *Technical Standard of the National System for Participative Planning*, https://www.planificacion.gob.ec/wp-content/uploads/downloads/2019/12/Norma_Tecnica_del_Sistema_Nacional_de_Planificacion_Participativa.pdf (accessed on 27 March 2021).

Box 2.8. The development and structure of the National Integrity and Anti-corruption Policy of Peru

The National Integrity and Anti-corruption Policy (*Política Nacional de Integridad y Lucha contra la Corrupción*), adopted with Decree N° 092-2017-PCM of September 14, 2017, is a state policy that encompasses all levels of government and public actors, constituting a guide and orientation for the private sector as well. The policy builds on the mandate of the Constitution and of other national strategic and development policies (*Acuerdo Nacional*; *Plan Bicentenario: el Perú hacia el 2021*; *Política Nacional de Modernización de la Gestión Pública*). Furthermore, the policy is linked to the implementation of the SDGs and other international instruments such as the UNCAC and the OAS Inter-American Convention against Corruption. It also confirms Peru´s commitment to participate in other international fora such as the OECD, the APEC, the CELAC and the Summit of Americas.

The development of the policy was co-ordinated by the High-level Commission against Corruption (CAN) – the national co-ordination mechanism on integrity and anti-corruption issues - and provides for a comprehensive diagnostic of corruption and its causes in Peru and defines three themes of priority actions: preventive capacity, risk identification and management, and enforcing capacity. Each of these themes consists of specific objectives with related responsibilities and guidelines. Furthermore, the policy defines minimum standards on various issues such as culture of integrity, conflict of interest and electoral systems, for example.

Source: Government of Peru (2017[30]), *National Integrity and Anti-corruption Policy*,
https://cdn.www.gob.pe/uploads/document/file/45986/Politica-Nacional-de-Integridad-y-Lucha-contra-la-Corrupcio%CC%81n.pdf
(accessed on 12 April 2021).

3 Strengthening the institutional arrangements for integrity in the Executive branch of Ecuador

This Chapter analyses the institutional arrangements for integrity within the Executive branch of Ecuador, highlighting the challenges in defining leadership and recognising the role of key actors in building a culture of integrity. It highlights that rather than creating a new ad-hoc Secretariat, Ecuador could leverage the co-ordination role of the General Secretariat of the Presidency of the Republic and the existing integrity-related competences of the Ministry of Labour. The Chapter also describes the composition and functions of the Ethics Committees and Anti-bribery Committees within public entities and provides an overview of integrity policies. It finds that both the Committees and policies do not embrace a preventive approach and that the units in charge of organisational change and culture could play a greater role in promoting and mainstreaming a culture of public integrity at entity-level.

Establishing clear responsibilities for leading and implementing integrity within the Executive branch

The institutional changes over the last years prevented the development of institutional leadership and the consolidation of sustainable integrity policies

The fragmented institutional context illustrated in Chapter 0 has also been affecting the development of an integrity leadership within the Executive branch. Starting from 2007, Ecuador has made several attempts to create a Secretariat within the Presidency of the Republic with responsibilities on integrity and anti-corruption-related issues. This included the (first) National Anti-corruption Secretariat (*Secretaría Nacional Anticorrupción*) in 2007, the National Secretariat for Management Transparency (*Secretaría Nacional de Transparencia de Gestión*) in 2008 and the National Secretariat of Public Administration (*Secretaría Nacional de la Administración Pública*) in 2013, whose responsibilities where then transferred to other Secretariats in 2017 (Box 3.1).

Box 3.1. Integrity and anti-corruption institutional changes within the Executive branch 2007-2017

By Executive Decree No. 122 of February 16, 2007, the government created the National Anti-Corruption Secretariat (*Secretaría Nacional Anticorrupción*) assigned to the Presidency of the Republic. It oversaw the government anti-corruption policy and developed strategies to investigate, determine and inform the competent authorities about acts of corruption. However, a few months later, through the Third Transitory Provision of the 2008 Constitution, the public officials of the National Anti-Corruption Secretariat, who had not been freely appointed, were transferred to the Council for Citizen Participation and Social Control.

Subsequently, through the Executive Decree No. 1511 of December 29, 2008, the government created the National Secretariat for Management Transparency (*Secretaría Nacional de Transparencia de Gestión*) within the Presidency. Its functions included: i) Investigate and denounce acts of corruption committed by public servants, and inform the Council for Citizen Participation and Social Control the result of the investigations, and ii) Strengthen the co-ordination and co-operation between government institutions, control bodies, judicial entities and all those involved in the investigation, prosecution and punishment of acts of corruption.

By Executive Decree No. 1522 of May 17, 2013, the National Secretariat for Management Transparency was transformed into Undersecretary's Office and merged by absorption into the National Secretariat of Public Administration (*Secretaría Nacional de la Administración Pública*).

Finally, by Executive Decree No. 5 of May 24, 2017, the National Secretariat of Public Administration was eliminated and its powers were transferred to the General Secretariat of the Presidency of the Republic (*Secretaría General de la Presidencia de la República*), the National Secretariat of Planning and Development (*Secretaría Nacional de Planeación y Desarrollo*), the Ministry of Telecommunications and the Information Society (*Ministerio de Telecomunicaciones y de la Sociedad de la Información*), and the Ministry of Labour (*Ministerio del Trabajo*), without making any specific mention of the powers related to the fight against corruption.

The latest institutional attempt to create an entity leading and co-ordinating integrity and anti-corruption efforts in the public administration was the creation, through Executive Decree No. 665 of February 6, 2019, of a new Anti-corruption Secretariat (*Secretaría Anticorrupción*), whose responsibilities included strengthening the co-operation between government institutions on anti-corruption matters. The Anti-corruption Secretariat was dissolved on 22 May 2020 through Executive Decree No. 1065 of May 21, 2020, without any formal handover of its leadership and co-ordination roles to any other institution. Currently, the General Secretariat of the Presidency of the Republic is responsible for related issues such as policies for public administration and open government and is co-ordinating some integrity and anti-corruption-related activities such as those related to this integrity report and, pursuant to Executive Decree No. 1212 of December 17, 2020, to the representation of the country in front of the Mechanism for the Implementation of the Inter-American Convention against Corruption (*Mecanismo de Seguimiento de la Implementación de la Convención Interamericana contra la Corrupción*, MESICIC). Nonetheless, Ecuador is yet to identify a leading entity for proposing, co-ordinating and promoting integrity policies for entities of the executive branch, which is one essential element to institutionalise integrity in the whole public administration.

The challenges in defining leadership in this area are also perceived as such by other actors as confirmed by the answers to the OECD questionnaire prepared to collect information from several public institutions and entities of the Executive branch. Indeed, most of them could not identify any mechanism to co-ordinate and implement integrity policies within the Executive branch. As for those institutions who provided an answer, reference was made to the Executive Decree No. 21 of 5 June 2017, which declared the strengthening of public policies' transparency and the fight against corruption as a priority government policy, or to the Presidential Provision No. 1343 and No. 1419 through which the Anti-Corruption Secretariat was given the responsibility to follow up and receive reports on the entities' progress in the implementation of the 37001 standard of the International Organization for Standardizationon (ISO) Anti-bribery management systems. This feedback was confirmed during the fact-finding mission, where institutions from the Executive branch highlighted the lack of awareness about the existence of any co-ordinating body on integrity issues after the dissolution of the Anti-corruption Secretariat.

Despite its role and responsibilities, the Ministry of Labour is not recognised as an integrity actor within the Executive branch

The lack of institutional leadership on integrity is paired with the underestimation of the role of other key integrity actors in Ecuador, both at the executive and country levels. This is especially the case of the Ministry of Labour, which is responsible for a broad range of policy areas, including many integrity-related ones such as meritocracy, professionalisation, capacity building, organisational culture, change-management, control of the public service and disciplinary enforcement.

There is a strong relationship between human resource management and public integrity and the *OECD Recommendation on Public Integrity* recognises the role of merit to build a culture of public integrity in organisations as one of the components of a public integrity system. It recommends that adherents "promote a merit-based, professional, public sector dedicated to public service values and good governance, in particular through:

- Ensuring human resource management that consistently applies basic principles, such as merit and transparency, to support the professionalism of the public service, prevents favouritism and nepotism, protects against undue political interference and mitigates risks for abuse of position and misconduct.
- Ensuring a fair and open system for recruitment, selection and promotion, based on objective criteria and a formalised procedure, and an appraisal system that supports accountability and a public service ethos". (OECD, 2017[6])

Indeed, meritocracy has been shown to reduce corruption (Charron et al., 2017[32]; Dahlström, Lapuente and Teorell, 2012[33]; Meyer-Sahling and Mikkelsen, 2016[34]). Furthermore, having merit systems in place reduces opportunities for patronage and nepotism, and provides the necessary foundations to develop a culture of integrity.

The Ministry of Labour has several responsibilities to promote human resource policies and a merit-based public administration as well as other aspects relevant to mainstreaming integrity throughout the public administration. According to the Organic Law of Public Service of October 6, 2010 (LOSEP), regulated by Executive Decree No. 710 of April 1, 2011, it is responsible, among others, for:

- Proposing State and Government policies related to the administration of human resources in the public sector.
- Carrying out control in the central and institutional administration of the Executive branch by means of inspections, verifications, supervisions or evaluation of administrative management.
- Managing the National Information System and the register of all public sector servants and entities.
- Establishing national policies and technical standards for training, as well as co-ordinating the implementation of training and education programmes.
- Requesting from the human resources units of the public administration, information related to human resources, salary and supplementary income.

Within the Ministry of Labour, the Under-secretariat for Meritocracy and Human Resources Development (*Subsecretaría de Meritocracia y Desarrollo del Talento Humano*) is particularly relevant in this context because its competence includes merit, human resources development, performance evaluation, training, and organisational culture. This is also reflected in its institutional mission, which is to develop a meritocratic system in the public service through the design and application of technical tools and the promotion of good practices in the processes of recruitment, human resources development and change management in the public service, to ensure the professionalisation and continuous improvement of public management in the application of the principles of efficiency, transparency, access to information and equal opportunities. The Under-Secretariat for Evaluation and Public Service Control is also relevant for public integrity because it is responsible for internal controls concerning compliance with the provisions of the LOSEP and other relevant regulations in order to promote the improvement of the institutional management of public service entities (Ministry of Labour of Ecuador, 2018[35]).

Furthermore, the Ministry of Labour is the governing body of the human resources units as well as of the organisational change and culture units within all public entities of the executive branch (*unidades de administración de talento humano* and *unidades de cambio y cultura organizacional*), making it particularly meaningful and crucial to mainstream integrity policies in the public administration since they are, in turn, responsible or have the role at the entity level for recruitment, management of performance, organisational culture and change management, code of ethics and ethics committees, training, and conflict of interest situations.

As part of the Open Government Action Plan 2019-2022, the Ministry of Labour is also responsible for the co-creation of a strategy with the participation and contributions of various actors for improving the quality of public services in the Executive branch based on the measurement resulting from the evaluations made by citizens, both from face-to-face and virtual channels.

Despite the role that the Ministry of Labour plays for public integrity, both in terms of policy development and implementation, the answers to the OECD questionnaire and the information shared during the fact-finding interviews evidence that it has never been involved in anti-corruption initiatives and it has been hardly identified as a key anti-corruption player neither in the Executive branch nor at the national level. This can be explained in part with the strong enforcement focus of anti-corruption initiatives in Ecuador, as well as with the broad competences of the Ministry of Labour, which is often associated with policies aimed at promoting employment in both the public and private sector.

To create an integrity system within the Executive branch, Ecuador could assign the General Secretariat of the Presidency of the Republic co-ordination and advisory functions while enhancing the role of the Ministry of Labour in the promotion of integrity standards and values

The analysis of information collected through the OECD questionnaire and fact-finding interviews highlighted that the lack of institutionalisation of integrity and anti-corruption efforts observed at the national level also concerns the Executive branch. Ecuador has not defined clear institutional arrangements and responsibilities for leading the integrity agenda and co-ordinating between various entities of the public administration. Plus, it has not sufficiently leveraged the role of all relevant actors in its strategy and efforts to mainstream integrity in public entities.

Indeed, any level and branch of the public administration include different actors with integrity responsibilities. This is the case for central, subnational or ministry levels of the administration but also for other branches of the state. In each of these dimensions, integrity actors are usually divided into "core" actors, such as the institutions, units or individuals responsible for implementing integrity policies and "complementary" actors, whose primary purpose is not to directly support the integrity system, but without whom the system could not operate (including functions such as finance, human resource management and public procurement) (Maesschalck and Bertok, 2009[36]). The specific assignments of responsibility depend on the institutional and legal context of each system that is considered. However, regardless of where the responsibilities are assigned, the actors performing integrity functions should have the appropriate level of authority to carry them out (OECD, 2020[12]).

Considering the challenges in the institutionalisation of integrity within the Executive branch, the government of Ecuador could clarify and assign integrity responsibilities by leveraging the roles and strengths of the existing institutional context, especially of the General Secretariat of the Presidency of the Republic and the Ministry of Labour.

First, the General Secretariat of the Presidency could be responsible for leading and co-ordinating the integrity agenda across the entities of the Executive branch, but also for advising the President of the Republic on legal or policy initiatives that could address challenges observed in its continuous interactions with public entities. These responsibilities of the General Secretariat of the Presidency would place the strategic leadership on integrity close to the President and thus demonstrate the highest commitment to promote integrity and fight corruption. At the same time, the General Secretariat of the Presidency would have the appropriate institutional role and authority to co-ordinate the integrity agenda of the government as well as the efforts of all other public institutions and entities belonging to the Executive branch through the Cabinet of Ministers. Furthermore, given the leading role envisaged for the President of the Republic in the National Integrity and Anti-corruption System, this would allow ensuring the essential coherence between the national strategy and the laws and policies adopted for the Executive branch.

Contrary to the responsibilities that were assigned to the Anti-corruption Secretariat, the General Secretariat of the Presidency should not assume a mandate that includes investigative tasks nor the reception of reports of possible corruption cases, which in turn differs from the General Secretariat of the Presidency's Citizens Directorate (*Dirección de Atención Ciudadana*) competence to hear citizens' questions and concerns. These investigative tasks should remain under the existing remit of control and enforcement authorities within the Judicial and the Transparency and Social Control branches. In this sense, the focus of responsibilities should be on advisory and co-ordinating tasks in line with the existing strategic and advisory role of the General Secretariat (Box 3.2). Given the potential synergies with other issues related to the public administration and open government, this function could be assigned to the Under-secretariat for Government Management (*Subsecretaría General de Gestión Gubernamental*) of the General Secretariat of the Presidency of the Republic.

Box 3.2. The strategic role of the General Secretariat of the Presidency of the Republic

The General Secretariat of the Presidency has broad responsibilities which include the following strategic and advisory tasks in support of the President of the Republic:

- dealing with the political and strategic aspects of the Presidency
- analysing areas, issues, facts and actors having political and strategic interest with the objective to guide and facilitate the decision-making by the President
- follow-up on areas, issues, facts and actors having political and strategic interest that have been prioritised by the President.

The General Secretary has the ranking of Minister, is member of the Presidential Cabinet and is appointed by the President. The responsibilities of the General Secretary include the co-ordination with the Presidential Cabinet, public sector authorities, and actors from private sector and civil society.

Source: Presidency of the Republic of Ecuador (2016[37]), Decree 1067 of 8 June 2016, https://www.presidencia.gob.ec/wp-content/uploads/downloads/2016/07/a1_decreto_1067.pdf (accessed on 12 April 2021).

Second, the government of Ecuador could enhance the role of the Ministry of Labour by assigning it a clear mandate to promote and support a culture of public integrity within the all the public institutions and entities of the Executive branch. As discussed, Ecuador does not currently have an entity with such responsibility, and the Ministry of Labour is best placed because it is the governing body on human resource management and policies, including the development of a merit-based civil service which is a key component to build a culture of integrity, as well as control, evaluation and institutional strengthening.

The Ministry of Labour also co-ordinates the human resources units as well as the organisational change and culture units of all public entities which already manage integrity-related policies such as the Code of Ethics, conflict of interest, organisational culture, change management, training and disciplinary enforcement. As such, the policies and initiatives promoted by the Ministry of Labour could be easily mainstreamed in the entities and processes of the public administration. Considering the current structure of the Ministry, the integrity competence could be assigned to the Under-secretariat for Meritocracy and Human Resources Development, whose name should also include a reference to integrity in order to formalise the mandate and build awareness about the role of the Ministry in integrity and anti-corruption issues.

As for the specific tasks, the Ministry of Labour could develop, promote and support policies and initiatives aimed at mainstreaming integrity values and standards through formal instruments such as codes but also training programmes and arrangements favouring a culture of integrity focused on prevention. It could also leverage its mandate on control and institutional strengthening to enhance the role and impact of related policies in the integrity systems at the entity level. The work of the Ministry of Labour should develop in coherence and co-operation with the General Secretariat of the Presidency, as well as maintain co-ordination with other entities governing other integrity-related functions or at-risk sectors both in the Executive and the Transparency and Social Control branches such as the Directorate of the National Public Procurement Service (*Directorio del Servicio Nacional de Contratación Pública*), the Office of the Comptroller General and the Ombudsman Office.

In designing the concrete role of the General Secretariat of the Presidency of the Republic and the Ministry of Labour, Ecuador could consider the institutional model adopted by Chile, which has similarities with the institutional and administrative set-up of Ecuador and which includes an advisory and co-ordination commission steered by the Presidency but also a civil service entity with a key role in promoting and mainstreaming integrity policies and 'systems' in the public sector entities (Box 3.3).

Box 3.3. The advisory, co-ordinating and culture of integrity's functions in the public integrity system of Chile

The leading institutions that generate public policies on matters related to the public integrity system of Chile are the Office of the Comptroller General of the Republic (CGR), the Ministry of Foreign Affairs (MINREL), the Public Integrity and Transparency Commission of the Ministry General Secretariat of the Presidency (MINSEGPRES), the Financial Market Commission (CMF), the State Defence Council (CDE), the Council for Transparency (CPLT), the Public Procurement and Contracting Directorate (CHILECOMPRA), the Judiciary (*Poder Judicial*), the Office of the Prosecutor General (*Fiscalía de Chile*), the Financial Analysis Unit (UAF), the Civil Service (*Servicio Civil*), and the Undersecretary of Regional and Administrative Development (*Subsecretaría de Desarrollo Regional y Administrativo*). Among those, two actors are particularly relevant in the present context:

- The **Ministerial Advisory Commission for Administrative Probity and Transparency in the Civil Service** (*Comisión Asesora Ministerial para la Probidad Administrativa y la Transparencia en la Función Pública*) is an advisory body of the Ministry General Secretariat of the Presidency, which provides advice to the Ministry on matters related to integrity and transparency in the civil service, and on co-ordination between the different bodies of the State Administration in matters related to compliance with the regulations on integrity.

- The **National Directorate of the Civil Service** (*Servicio Civil*) is responsible for the implementation of policies on the management and development of public officials and the senior management. As part of this mission, it provides Ministries and public entities with guidance to develop codes of ethics and to establish integrity systems at entity level. The National Directorate of the Civil Service has been supporting the development and implementation of participatory codes of ethics as well as the implementation and monitoring of integrity systems based on codes of ethics. On top of this guiding role, it also prepares an annual report on the implementation of integrity systems in the whole public sector.

The National Directorate of the Civil Service also has the mandate to build capacity and promote compliance with standards of integrity and transparency in public entities. Trainings are carried out on a regular basis for public officials, especially for those who perform co-ordination functions on integrity issues. In 2019, officials participating in these training activities amounted to around 2000. In parallel, the Civil Service has been working with UNDP and the UNCAC's Anti-corruption Alliance on an online interactive course that includes two areas - civic training modules on integrity and training modules on integrity systems and codes of ethics. Plus, ad-hoc tailored trainings have been organised in co-operation with institutions such as Chilecompra, the Financial Analysis Unit, Comptroller's Office, and State Defence Council. Guidance and training have also been developed for entities at the subnational level, such as on the participatory development of code of ethics in municipalities.

In performing their respective roles and functions, these two actors have closely collaborated, for instance in the development and adoption of the Ordinance 2305 of 2018 on "Recommendations for the implementation and mainstreaming of the integrity system in the entities of the public administration". Plus, they have also collaborated with other relevant actors of the public integrity system of Chile, leading to initiatives such as the Compendium of Legal Acts on Integrity and Public Ethics that has been jointly prepared by the Comptroller General Office and the National Directorate of the Civil Service.

Source: (Anticorruption Alliance of Chile, n.d.[38]); (Ministerial Advisory Commission for Administrative Probity and Transparency in the Civil Service of Chile; National Directorate of the Civil Service of Chile;, 2018[39]); (National Directorate of the Civil Service of Chile; Comptroller General Office of Chile, 2017[40]); (National Directorate of the Civil Service of Chile, n.d.[41]).

Building integrity systems at the organisational level

Public entities in the Executive branch have adopted different institutional arrangements on integrity, but their function is mostly focused on assessing and sanctioning misconducts

One of the most significant challenges that countries face in developing a culture of public integrity is to effectively implement national regulations and policies at the level of public entities, where the organisational culture takes form and public integrity becomes part of behaviour of public officials. Although they play a different role and function, public sector entities also have a responsibility in mainstreaming existing integrity policies in their organisation by establishing and institutionalising an internal integrity system featuring key functions, regardless of the mandate. Table 3.1 provides an overview of these essential functions along with the position or unit that is responsible for their implementation in the experience of OECD countries.

Table 3.1. Actors and integrity roles forming an integrity system at the organisational level

Position or unit	Integrity role
Highest officer	Ultimately responsible for the agenda, implementation and enforcement of integrity policies for the entire organisation. Responsible for adhering to and demonstrating the highest levels of commitment and conduct for public integrity.
Management	Responsible for implementation of integrity policies and for promoting ethical behaviour within the organisational units for which they are responsible. Responsible for adhering to and demonstrating the highest levels of commitment and conduct for public integrity.
Integrity officer Integrity co-ordinator Compliance officer Integrity policy staff	A wide range of different types of officers who fulfil roles relating to: design, support and advice, implementation, co-operation, and enforcement of integrity policies.
Internal audit and control	Responsible for establishing an internal control system and risk management framework to reduce vulnerability to fraud and corruption and for ensuring that governments are operating optimally to deliver programmes that benefit citizens.
Finance	Responsible for taking care of vulnerable actions around purchasing, tenders, and expense claims in a transparent manner.
Legal	Responsible for formulating administrative-legal policy, providing advice based on relevant legislation and the drafting of delegation and mandate regulations, and applying an integrity lens to ensure policies comply with integrity standards.
Human resource management	Responsible for establishing procedures and providing advice concerning recruitment and selection, job descriptions, performance and assessment interviews, disciplinary research, sanctions and organisational culture, and applying an integrity lens to ensure processes comply with integrity standards.
Communication / Information	Responsible for communication concerning integrity standards and procedures.
Security/ICT	Responsible for setting up physical and ICT security.
Confidential advisor	Responsible for advising employees on and coaching them in the internal reporting process in the event of suspected integrity violations.

Source: OECD (2020[12]), *OECD Public Integrity Handbook*, OECD Publishing, Paris, https://doi.org/10.1787/ac8ed8e8-en.

Ecuador has taken steps to institutionalise integrity through the establishment of Ethics Committees and the adoption of the international standard ISO 37001 on the Anti-Bribery Management System.

Ethics Committees and Code

The obligation to establish an Ethics Committee in each public entity has been introduced by Resolution 2 of May 7, 2013 (published in Official Supplement Register 960 of May 23, 2013). They have the responsibility of receiving, knowing, investigating and resolving any possible violation of the Code of Ethics for Good Living of the Executive branch (*Código de Ética para el Buen Vivir de la Función Ejecutiva*, or Code of Ethics), as well as implementing and disseminating the Code within the entity. The Code is mandatory for all public officials of the Executive branch since 2013 and its purpose is to establish and promote ethical principles, values, responsibilities and commitments to achieve institutional objectives and contribute to the efficient use of public resources. The Code establishes a list of ethical principles and values such as integrity, transparency, quality, solidarity, collaboration, effectiveness, respect, responsibility, and loyalty. In addition, it defines the responsibilities related to the Code (Table 3.2) for members of the Ethics Committee, who are:

- Strategic Management Co-ordinator (presides and can vote)
- Highest authority or delegate (can intervene and vote)
- Two public officials, and two substitutes (can intervene and vote)
- Human Resources Director (can intervene but not vote)
- Legal Co-ordinator (who intervenes but does not vote).

Table 3.2. Responsibilities for members of the Ethics Committees

	Key Responsibilities
All members	- Implement and disseminate the Code of Ethics within the entity and at the different decentralised levels. - Recognise and encourage positive ethical behaviour. - In the case of possible breaches that may have civil or criminal law relevance, check any breach of the Code of Ethics and transmit it to the competent internal body with proposed solution. - Propose mediation between involved parties. - Make proposals for the updating and permanent improvement of the Code of Ethics.
Strategic Management Co-ordinator	- Set up the first Code of Ethics Committee. - Lead the organisation and operation of the Ethics Committee and define its procedure. - Gather observations on the Code of Ethics annually and make proposals for its updating and improvement. - Comply with and enforce the Code. - Promote the development of guiding documents with practical examples.
Highest authority	- Propose recommendations that give rise to suggestions in the cases. - Propose improvements and internal processes.
Human Resources Director	- Provide advice in areas related to human resources management. - Consider the suggestions in the final reports made by the Ethics Committee for each case.
Legal Co-ordinator	- Provide legal advice. - Drafting final reports.
National Secretariat for Management Transparency (now dissolved)	- Co-ordinate the Extended Ethics Committee to be held every six months with the entities of the Executive branch. - Monitor and evaluate the functioning of the Ethics Committees. - Propose improvements to the Code of Ethics. - Advise and train the institutions together with the National Civil Service Secretariat and the Ministry of Labour on the ethical performance of their entities.

Source: Ministry of Health of Ecuador (2012[42]), *Code of Ethics for Good Living of the Executive branch*, https://issuu.com/saludecuador/docs/doc_codigo_etica (accessed on 12 April 2021).

Entities such as the Presidency of the Republic (*Presidencia de la Republica*), the Ministry of Transportation and Public Works (*Ministerio de Transporte y Obras Públicas*), the Ministry of Environment (*Ministerio de Ambiente y Agua*) and the Ministry of Labour issued ministerial agreements (No. SGPR-2014-0002, No. 067 of 30 July 2013, No. 079 of April 23, 2014, and No. 0133 MRL-2013, respectively) for the conformation of their Institutional Ethics Committees, and the definition of their own values and principles along with the ones of the national Code of Ethics. In addition, these agreements provide a list of concrete actions that the public officials are required to observe for the application of the principles and values of their respective Codes. For instance, the National Public Procurement Service (*Servicio Nacional de Contratación Pública*), updated its Ethics Committee through Internal Resolution No. RI-SERCOP-2019-00004 and its Code of Ethics, through Internal Resolutions No. R.I.-SERCOP-2019-00005 and R.I.-SERCOP-2019-00008, establishing expected behaviours and specific prohibitions for the daily exercise of the functions of its officials. Some decentralised autonomous governments have also established Ethics Committees, for example in the Province of Pichincha, which established one consisting of the Provincial Prefect, the Director of Human Resources Management and Administration as well as two representatives of the public officials.

Although several institutions have an Ethics Committee in place, the requirement has been modified in 2016 through Ministerial Agreement No. 0001606 of 17 May 2016, which decided to simplify such Committees by assigning the responsibility to monitor and ensure the implementation and enforcement of the Code of Ethics to the human resources units of each public entity.

The Anti-corruption and Transparency Management Committees pursuant to standard ISO 37001

Following the 2019 Presidential Annual Address to the Nation (Presidency of the Republic of Ecuador, 2019[43]), public entities have also been required to implement the Anti-bribery 37001 standard of the International Organization for Standardization (ISO), which includes, among others, the creation of an Anti-corruption body in each entity. (Box 3.4) For this purpose, the former Anti-Corruption Secretariat entered into inter-institutional agreements with seven public companies (the Co-ordinating Company of Public Companies, the National Electricity Corporation, the Electric Corporation of Ecuador, the National Telecommunications Corporation, the Ecuadorian Oil Fleet, Petroamazonas and Petroecuador) as well as with municipal entities to support the implementation of this standard. Other public entities of the Executive such SERCOP, the Ministry of Economy and Finance, the Ministry of Production, Foreign Trade, Investment and Fisheries (*Ministerio de Producción, Comercio Exterior, Inversiones y Pesca*) have adopted the ISO 37001 standard and others are in the process of doing so. To adopt the ISO standard, public entities seek support from specialised consulting companies and must be certified by one of the two authorised companies in Ecuador every 3 years. Public entities can choose to certify the organisation as a whole or specific areas or procedures. Both the adoption and the certification process comes along with a cost for the public entities. In addition to the certification process, some interviews during the fact-finding mission mentioned that public entities report on activities and results related to the implementation of the standards to the Presidency of the Republic. However, it not clear whether this is an obligation for all public entities having adopted the standard and whether this information is analysed or used to monitor its implementation or any other purpose.

Box 3.4. The ISO 37001 standard and the contribution of Ecuador in its development

The ISO 37001 standard of 2016 specifies requirements and provides guidance for establishing, implementing, maintaining, reviewing and improving an anti-bribery management system. In addition, it refers to several measures to help organisations prevent and detect bribery. It applies to all organisations, irrespective of their type, size and nature of business or activity, whether in the public, private or not-for-profit sectors.

The standard aims to support entities in the implementation of reasonable and proportionate measures to prevent bribery. These measures include management leadership, training, risk assessment, due process, financial and business controls, reporting, auditing and investigation.

The Ecuadorian Standardization Service, the public technical body of the National Quality System and member of ISO (International Organization for Standardization) for Ecuador, was designated as co-ordinator and participated in its drafting within the "Mirror Committee of the ISO 37001 Standard". Together with other Spanish-speaking countries such as Colombia, Argentina or Mexico, it also contributed to the official translation.

Source: Ecuadorian Standardization Service (n.d.[44]), *The adoption of the ISO 37001 will help define anti-corruption strategies*, https://www.normalizacion.gob.ec/la-adopcion-de-la-norma-iso-37001-permitira-definir-estrategias-contra-la-corrupcion/ (accessed on 12 April 2021)

Taking as example the Anti-corruption Committee created by the Ministry of Economy and Finance pursuant to standard ISO 37001, its mission is to steer and monitor the Institutional Anti-bribery Management System of the entity. The body is composed of the following members:

- The General Financial Administrative Co-ordinator (or delegate), who chairs the Committee.
- The permanent delegate of the Minister of Economy and Finance.
- The General Legal Co-ordinator (or delegate), who shall act as Secretary.
- The Deputy Ministers of Economy and Finance (or delegate).
- The General Co-ordinator of Planning and Strategic Management (or delegate).

The implementing regulation defines the responsibilities of the body, as well as of the Chair and Secretary. It also establishes the functions and responsibilities of the Committee, which include:

- Approving the internal regulations for the operation of the Anti-Bribery Management System and, in general, those related to the fight against corruption in the entity.
- Resolving the reports that the Chairman of the Committee presents in the plenary of the Committee.
- Reviewing the monthly report on the status of the reports received and issuing directives and guidelines for administrative investigation on them, without prejudice to the judicial enforcement.
- Periodically reviewing the risks determined by the Anti-Bribery Management System as well as approving updates to the risk management methodology.
- Ensuring compliance with all requirements set out in the processes of the Anti-Bribery Management System.
- Ensure the communication of the institutional Anti-Bribery Policy through the institution's communication media as well as the regulations and procedures generated within the System.

- Take the necessary actions to prevent retaliation, discrimination, disciplinary action, reporting or any other administrative action against any member of the institution or third party(ies) who has made submitted a report.
- Periodically reporting to the head of the institution on Anti-Bribery Management System and of bribery reports that have identified as serious or systematic.

Lastly, the regulation also adopts a programme on integrity (Box 3.5) and another one on anti-bribery, which are also the responsibility of the Anti-corruption Committee.

Box 3.5. The integrity programme of the Ministry of Economy and Finance based on standard ISO 37001

The Integrity Programme of the Ministry of Economy and Finances aims to support the implementation of a series of measures and actions aimed at preventing, controlling and managing any possible risk of committing corrupt conducts to which the institution is exposed in its operations. The responsibility of its implementation is with the Anti-corruption Committee, in co-ordination, when relevant, with the Institutional Transparency Committee.

The programme foresees a "management system" monitoring and evaluation the Plan as well as the implementation of a risk-management system and of a conflict of interest management system as well as the promotion of institutional capacity for prevention together with communication and capacity-building activities. The plan refers to the review of the Code of Ethics, sets certain prohibitions in relation to facilitation payments and gifts, and affirms the principle of transparency. Lastly, it provides for the development of protocols allowing public officials and private actors to file complaints in the event of fraudulent or corrupt acts, clearly specifying how to file a complaint, the requirements, the channels for filing complaints, the protection measures for those submit the complaints and those responsible for their reception.

Source: Ministry of Economy and Finance of Ecuador (2019[45]), (2019), *Standards on the Fight against Corruption and the Anti-bribery Management System in the Ministry of Economy and Finance*, https://www.finanzas.gob.ec/wp-content/uploads/downloads/2019/07/Acuerdo-Lucha-Contra-la-Corrupci%C3%B3n.pdf (accessed on 12 April 2021).

Ecuador could give the mandate to promote and co-ordinate integrity and other preventive initiatives to the organisational change and culture units within public entities

Next to these institutional and co-ordination efforts, several laws and policies in Ecuador are supporting public integrity. While each of these laws and policies calls for an in-depth review in terms of their scope and implementation, also to identify potential overlaps or gaps, the fact-finding interviews provided the general indication that few of them embrace a preventive approach and contribute to building an organisational culture of integrity.

Considering the focus of the present report and following the structure of the *OECD Recommendation* (OECD, 2017[6]), the analysis made in the present section focuses on assessing the institutional grounding of key integrity laws and policies at the level of public entities. Indeed, to be effective integrity laws and policies need to be institutionalised and implemented at the entity level and thereby mainstreamed throughout the public administration (OECD, 2019[1]).

Managing conflict of interests and asset declarations

> *The OECD Recommendation calls for "...setting clear and proportionate procedures (...) to manage actual or potential conflicts of interest" and to provide "easily accessible formal and informal guidance and consultation mechanisms to help public officials apply public integrity standards in their daily work as well as to manage conflict-of-interest situations". (OECD, 2017[6])*

In Ecuador, the Organic Law of the Public Service (*Ley Orgánica del Servicio Público*) No. 294 of 6 October 2010, which is complemented by the Executive Decree No. 710 of April 1, 2011, includes some relevant prohibitions on designation, appointment and contracting in public entities. It also establishes the responsibilities and penalties in case of non-compliance, special prohibitions for the performance of a position in the public sector and others in the case of multi-employment.

With regards to declarations, two of the requirements for entering a public position are the presentation of a sworn statement (*declaración juramentada*) stating that the candidate it is not found incurred on legal grounds of impediment, disability or prohibition for the exercise of a public office, as well as the presentation of the corresponding sworn asset declaration (*declaración patrimonial juramentada*). As established in article 3 of the Organic Law of the Public Service, public officials are required to present the asset declaration at the beginning and at the end of their working period and to update it every two years. The Law established that the information contained in the declarations is public and that the lack of presentation of the declaration at the beginning of the working period will result in the immediate cancellation of the appointment or contract and the termination of duties, in addition to the removal of the head of the human resources management unit who has recruited the public official without that requirement. Furthermore, according to the Organic Law for the Application of the Popular Consultation of February 19, 2017, it is prohibited for citizens to enter the public service while owning assets in countries which are considered as tax havens.

The Office of the Comptroller General of the State (*Contraloría General del Estado*, CGE) defines the format and procedures for the asset declarations of public officials. In the public entities, the human resources management units in each institution are responsible for verifying that the declarations have been submitted to the CGE, which carries out the review of the declarations and the processes of verification of the information to identify possible cases of illicit enrichment.

Capacity building

> The OECD Recommendation calls for providing "sufficient information, training, guidance and timely advice for public officials to apply public integrity standards in the workplace", in particular by "offering induction and on-the-job integrity training to public officials throughout their careers in order to raise awareness and develop essential skills for the analysis of ethical dilemmas, and to make public integrity standards applicable and meaningful in their own personal contexts". (OECD, 2017[6])

In Ecuador, training and capacity building activities on integrity-related issues are managed by each single entity and are usually linked to the Code of Ethics. Examples include:

- The Ministry of Health (*Ministerio de Salud Pública*) has been organising various virtual courses and workshops on the Code of Ethics in the last five years and it is planned to develop new training methodologies in 2021.

- The National Human Resources Directorate of the Internal Revenue Service (*Servicio de Rentas Internas*) offers courses related to integrity and ethics in its annual institutional training plan. In the last three years they offered activities on control pursuant to the Organic Law of Public Service, ethics, professional ethics in public administration, public ethics, as well as institutional reputation and identity.

- The National Public Procurement Service has an internal workshop course on the ISO 37001 standard, which has been running since 2019 and has so far had four editions and the participation of 688 civil servants.

- The Ministry of Economy and Finance developed a training programme linked to its anti-bribery management system. It should be approved by all the Ministry's civil servants, including the highest authority. As of October 2020, 537 civil servants have been trained.

Answers from the OECD questionnaire also mentioned that issues of transparency, ethics and integrity are addressed as part of the induction training for new public officials. Indeed, according to the Technical Standard of the Training and Capacity Building Sub-System (*Norma Técnica del Subsistema de Formación y Capacitación*) these trainings are delivered by the Human Talent Management Unit (*Unidad de Administración de Talento Humano*, UATH) of each institution and are meant to raise awareness on principles and values in accordance with the specific vision, mission and goals of each institution. Furthermore, the Ministry of Labour has established the "Executives of Excellence" programme, a merit-based initiative that promotes the selection of candidates with managerial skills to fill executive positions (*Nivel Jerárquico Superior*, NJS) following the principles of suitability, transparency, and equitability (OECD, forthcoming[4]). Moreover, the Office of the Comptroller General organises a relevant training programme on "public ethics, citizen participation and social control" which includes courses for citizens and public officials. This programme addresses conceptual, normative and methodological aspects on public management control, social control and citizen participation, the social role of the Office of the Comptroller General and issues related to public ethics. According to the Annual Institutional Training Plan 2019, 55 training courses have been organised on those topics, involving 3 372 public officials in both in-person and virtual format (UNDOC, 2020[20]).

Answers to the OECD questionnaire also mentioned the role that the Anti-Corruption Secretariat had in supporting capacity building initiatives and that no other institution has succeeded in that after its dissolution. Indeed, the follow-up interviews during fact-finding mission confirmed the existence of capacity building activities offered by some institutions, but also that the lack of an entity promoting a uniform and harmonised approach on capacity building results in a fragmented and uneven activities thorough the public entities of the executive branch.

Open culture and whistle-blower protection

> The OECD Recommendation calls for encouraging "an open culture where ethical dilemmas, public integrity concerns, and errors can be discussed freely", to provide "clear rules and procedures for reporting suspected violations of integrity standards, and ensure (...) protection in law and practice against all types of unjustified treatments as a result of reporting in good faith and on reasonable grounds" and to provide "alternative channels for reporting suspected violations of integrity standards, including when appropriate the possibility of confidentially reporting to a body with the mandate and capacity to conduct an independent investigation." (OECD, 2017[6])

The answers to the OECD questionnaire in Ecuador provided different views regarding institutional space where public officials can turn to openly discuss doubts and concerns related to integrity such as ethical dilemmas situation or conflict of interest situations. Most institutions pointed out to the human resources and legal units, but also to the immediate superior or the Ethics Committee. With regards to initiatives promoting an open organisational culture, those that have been mentioned include:

- Focus groups for the discussion of doubts and concerns about the work environment in reference to institution's strategy and the results obtained in the work climate survey.
- Virtual tools such as the one called "*Buzón Cuéntame*", through which public officials can make contributions, suggestions, comments, acknowledgements regarding the work environment of the institution and other issues.
- Annual performance evaluations that include questions on the participation of employees in the management and decision-making of their administrative unit and the entity in general.
- Work climate and organisational culture surveys with room for comments and suggestions.

Although these are useful initiatives to improve organisational culture and well-being, the interviews during the fact-finding mission confirmed there is no specific unit or area with mandate for promoting an open organisational culture, as understood in *OECD Recommendation on Public Integrity* (OECD, 2017[6]). They also highlighted that the indicated channels are not commonly used by public officials to seek for ethical advice. This is due in part to the fact that most of those areas have a competence on investigative or disciplinary issues, which does not create the right environment to have open discussion.

In turn, regulations and guidelines for the submission of complaints are in place in Ecuador, but for all citizens in general. The Regulation for the Presentation, Reception and Processing of Complaints for Administrative Investigation in the Office of the Comptroller General was adopted through Agreement 045-CG-2018 of 27 July 2018 along with the following key points:

- Simplification of requirements for the submission of complaints.
- Setting up a wider variety of channels to submit complaints: in writing, verbally, by telephone, by e-mail, and via the institutional website.
- Ensuring confidentiality of information to bona fide complainants in order to guarantee the protection of their personal data.

The Council for Citizen Participation and Social Control also established a regulation for the management of requests and complaints about acts or omissions that affect participation or generate corruption (Resolution No. PLE-CPCCS-022-26-11-2015).

Some public entities such as the Ministry of Economy and Finance and the Ministry of Production, Foreign Trade, Investment and Fisheries, the Internal Revenue Service and SERCOP have set up their own internal whistleblowing policies and protocols in the framework of the ISO 37001. Outside the executive branch, the Office of the Prosecutor General has also set up an on-line tool called Transparency Inbox (*Buzón Transparencia*) where citizens can report alleged acts of corruption and irregularities committed by its public officials.

The different but related mechanism of protection of witnesses and victims in criminal proceedings is provided by the Office of the Prosecutor General through the National System for Victim and Witness Protection (*Sistema Nacional de Protección de Víctimas y Testigos*). Protection may be afforded to the families of participants in criminal proceedings, but not to other persons close to witnesses or experts; only the prosecutor, not the persons seeking protection, may apply for protective measures.

While efforts have been taken, especially in some public entities, Ecuador lacks a national whistleblowing policy and mechanism which is tailored to public officials and that also includes effective protection against reprisals. This a crucial feature to promote the use of whistleblowing, as also stressed by the *OECD Recommendation on Public Integrity* (OECD, 2017[6]).

Risk management and audit

> The OECD Recommendation call for applying "an internal control and risk management framework to safeguard integrity in public sector organisations" as well to "reinforce the role of external oversight and control within the public integrity system." (OECD, 2017[6])

The Office of the Comptroller General of the State (*Contraloría General del Estado*, CGE) is the Supreme Audit Institution of Ecuador and has the Constitutional mandate to control the use of State resources and the achievement of the goals of State institutions and private-law legal entities that dispose of government resources (Art. 211). The responsibilities of the CGE include the direction of the administrative control system, comprised of internal auditing, external auditing and internal control of public sector institutions (as defined in Art. 225 and 315 of the Constitution) and those private-sector entities that dispose of government resources.

These entities are required to follow the internal control standards defined by the Comptroller General Office in 2009 (*Normas de control interno para las entidades, organismos del sector público y de las personas jurídicas de derecho privado que dispongan de recursos públicos*). They define internal control objectives and responsibilities, and set standards that guide entities, among other issues, on the control environment, control activities, and risk management. The Organic Law of the State Comptroller General

(*Ley Orgánica de la Contraloría General del Estado*), in its Art. 14, requires that each public entity, where justified, shall have an organised, independent and well-resourced Internal Audit Unit (*Unidad de Auditoría Interna*) to carry out *ex post* internal audits and provide timely and professional advice in the field of its competence, adding value to institutional management and reasonable assurance that the management of the highest authority and other public officials is carried out in accordance with the rules. The Internal Audit Units depend technically and administratively on the CGE and their organisation, structure, functions and attributions are further regulated in Agreement No. 59-CG-2018 of the CGE.

Although the risk management and internal control standards are comprehensive and aligned with international standards, in practice, the level of implementation seems to be limited. Interviews during the fact-finding mission highlighted that in particular the risk-management approach is limited within public entities, especially, but not only, in relation to integrity and corruption risks. Furthermore, the Internal Audit Units, when they exist, tend to focus on their audit function aimed at compliance with Laws and regulations, rather than providing independent, objective assurance and advice to the entity's management. In addition, similar to the case of Peru (OECD, 2017[46]), given that the Internal Audit Units depend technically and administratively on the CGE, there is a risk of generating confusion amongst public servants with respect to internal and external audit and control, and therefore their own role in guaranteeing an effective implementation of internal controls (OECD, 2019[1]).

Disciplinary enforcement

> The OECD Recommendation calls to "ensure that enforcement mechanisms provide appropriate responses to all suspected violations of public integrity standards by public officials and all others involved in the violations."

In Ecuador, the disciplinary regime is regulated by the Public Service Organic Law, whose Article 41 establishes that any public official who fails to comply with his or her obligations or who contravenes the provisions of this Law, incurs administrative liability and can lead to a disciplinary sanction. Disciplinary offences are divided into minor ones – such as failure to comply with working hours during a working day, inappropriate performance of activities during working hours – and serious ones, which are actions or omissions that seriously contravene the legal system or seriously alter the institutional order. Minor offences give rise to the imposition of verbal or written warning, an administrative pecuniary sanction or a fine. Sanctions for serious misconduct include the suspension or dismissal of the public official.

The administrative summary procedure (*sumario administrativo*) to ascertain disciplinary liability and eventually impose the corresponding sanctions is carried out by the Ministry of Labour through the human resources management unit of the public entity. The procedure should respect the due process guarantees, ensure the participation of the parties involved, respect for the right to defence and the *in dubio pro reo* principle.

Based on this preliminary review of some key laws and policies in Ecuador with relevance for public integrity, the following shortcomings emerge both in terms of scope and implementation at entity levels:

- The integrity system of public entities in the executive branch of Ecuador consists of institutional arrangements and policies which are mostly designed to discover and sanction corruption breaches. In the case of the Ethics Committees, their main function is to review possible breaches of the Code of Ethics, while for the ISO 37001 the focus is on bribery cases, which is narrower and closer to the criminal domain.

- Although differences exist among entities, a similar approach emerges from the analysis of the integrity policies applicable in entities and their implementation. In this sense, codes and rules on conflict of interest situations are conceived as legal tools to detect misconducts and the corresponding training offer is not homogenous and continuous for all public officials across the public institutions and public entities.

- Spaces for integrity advice and open discussions are limited and not used in practice, while the lack of protection for whistleblowers limits the submission of reports from those who experience a breach of integrity but fear reprisals at the workplace.

- Standards for risk management and internal control exist but their implementation in practice seems to be limited and do not target corruption and integrity risks. Internal audit formally depends on the CGE, and focuses more on *ex post* control rather than on providing assurance and support to management on the internal control and risk management environment. As the Internal Audit Units belong formally to the CGE, there is also a risk of creating confusion between internal and external audit and control.

- The disciplinary framework is in place, but challenges seem to exist in relation to its perceived effectiveness among public officials. Furthermore, the competence of the human resource management unit on disciplinary enforcement prevents public officials to turn to it for integrity-related questions such as ethical doubts or dilemmas.

The model proposed by the ISO 37001 standard covers relevant areas and issues, with some reference to the preventive perspective, and it may represent a tool to define and implement anti-corruption responsibilities and processes in public entities, as it has been the case in some of the public institutions and entities which that took part in the data-collection exercise. However, its sustainability and impact on institutionalising integrity at entity level seem to be limited by several factors and similar views on the strengths and weaknesses of the ISO 37001 standard have been raised in relation to its use in the private sector (Murphy, 2019[47]).

- First, the scope focuses on bribery, which is a criminally relevant offence whose scope is much narrower and conceptually different to public integrity, which refers to the "consistent alignment of, and adherence to, shared ethical values, principles and norms for upholding and prioritising the public interest over private interests in the public sector". (OECD, 2017[6])

- Second, as mentioned above, the ISO 37001 standard requires an external certification process that may create a positive incentive for the entity to comply with it, but cannot be intended as a guarantee that the entity is immune from integrity and corruption risks. Concerns have been raised in this sense during various interviews of the fact-finding mission, where it was pointed out that there is a risk that the certification is used by entities as an end in itself for mere communication and reputation purposes. This may impair the development of a sustainable integrity system, which requires continued commitment and substantial efforts aiming at building a culture of integrity. A highly-publicised certification that is not backed by changes or continued scandals can even backfire and further fuel mistrust in government's anti-corruption efforts.

- Similarly, it was pointed out that the certification implies costs that need to be covered with public funds, has to be renewed on a recurrent basis and can only be carried out by two external companies, which may create the perception of limited competition for such delicate role requiring the highest degree of independence and the perception thereof.

Considering these limits and uneven results of existing institutional models in creating cultures of integrity throughout the public administration, Ecuador could decide to focus the function of both the Ethics Committees and the Anti-bribery Committee on enforcement-related matters, including the review of possible breaches of the Code of Ethics. This is one of the main responsibilities of these Committees, and the one they are most known for by public officials.

In addition, it could assign the integrity mandate with a clear preventive approach to another unit within public entities that is not associated with investigations or enforcement functions. Considering the current institutional environment of public entities in the Executive branch and the importance of linking the concept of public integrity to already defined units and responsibilities, Ecuador could assign it to the organisational change and culture units (*unidades de cambio y cultura organizacional*) or whoever perform their functions. These are generally in charge of proposing, implementing, leading and managing transformation and change management processes of organisational culture and institutional reform, which can also be leveraged to promote and develop a culture of integrity. (Box 3.6) These units could support in the participatory development of standards, provide clarifications and confidential advice on integrity issues - also from questions or results of the organisational culture surveys -, organise participative debate and discussions on ethical topics emerging from the advice function and surveys, as well as promote and contribute to the capacity building activities on integrity.

Box 3.6. Organisational change and culture units in Ecuador

The organisational change and culture units usually belong to the area that in public entities is responsible for strategic management and their main objective is to lead change management processes inside the organisations in view of achieving continuous development of organisational culture and institutional maturity.

The specific tasks attributed to these units vary depending on the entity. However, taking as an example those established in the Ministry of Health and the Ministry of Education, they are commonly responsible to develop, among others, the following products:

- Climate and culture measurement reports.
- Proposals for change management and innovation projects and programmes.
- Action plans for improvement of the organisational climate and culture.
- Awareness raising and communication plans on change management and resilience as well as on innovation issues to generate a sense of belonging in the institution.
- Change management policies and tools to establish and maintain institutional communication.
- Communication and change management training plans to ensure an adequate flow of information to all staff.
- Reports on the implementation of organisational culture change management plans and programmes in the institution, to translate organisational strategies into concrete plans, monitor their execution and provide a complete overview of the management and performance of operation.
- Progress reports on the implementation of the Institutional Public Management Model.

Source: (Ministry of Health of Ecuador, n.d.[48]); (Ministry of Education of Ecuador, 2014[49]).

Mandating the organisational change and culture units, or whoever perform their functions, with an integrity mandate would be coherent with the recommended enhanced role of the Ministry of Labour in the integrity system at level of the executive function. Its Undersecretariat for Meritocracy and Human Resources Development (*Subsecretaría de Meritocracia y Desarrollo del Talento Humano*) also includes the Directorate for Change Management and Organisational Culture (*Dirección de Gestión del Cambio y Cultura Organizacional*), whose responsibilities include co-ordinating with the relevant units at the entity level the implementation of policies, methodological guidelines and tools necessary to manage actions focused on change management, climate, organisational culture and development of human resources management.

A crucial aspect that the OECD has been highlighting is to avoid that those units in public entities with an integrity mandate also receive and process report on possible corruption breaches, as it would create confusion and duplication with those units which already have such responsibility (OECD, 2019[50]). Indeed, adding an integrity mandate to the organisational change and culture units would give them a key role in the integrity system of the entity, but not the responsibility for all integrity-related areas. Its main function would be to promote and articulate relevant initiatives across the entity with the essential support of the highest authority and in close co-ordination with the ethics and anti-bribery committees but also the transparency and open data committees and all the other actors or areas that have relevant responsibilities in relation to human resources, training, transparency, open government, internal control and audit, risk management, investigations, and sanctions. In this context, Ecuador could consider the institutional models for institutional integrity adopted in Peru and Chile, which also feature an integrity function whose main responsibilities include the facilitation, co-ordination and promotion of integrity efforts and initiatives within the entity (Box 3.7).

Box 3.7. The integrity articulation and promotion function in public entities of Chile and Peru

The integrity system in Chile has been strengthened through the agendas of the different governments in office from 1994, developing more than 200 administrative and legal measures in matters of probity. Furthermore, a behavioural and participatory approach has also been introduced from 2015 onwards.

The guidance of the Presidential Advisory Council against conflicts of interest, influence peddling and corruption was considered in the 2016 "Agenda for Transparency and Probity in Business and Politics", and the dimensions of integrity and transparency have been constantly included in the subsequent presidential agendas. Some of the objectives of the Agenda include:

- Having an institutional code of ethics and ensuring compliance with it.
- Ensuring integrity strategies that count with the leadership of the senior head of service.
- Developing information channels, channels for consultation and channels for reporting of ethical breaches.

In order to achieve these objectives a formal structure is also recommended for the design and implementation of the integrity system. It includes the head of the entity, technical advisor(s), an integrity co-ordinator, an integrity committee and an integrity management platform. As of October 2020, 87% of public entities at the central level had established such structure, and 284 public institutions have built participatory codes of ethics.

In this context, it is relevant to highlight the role of the integrity co-ordinator, which is responsible for the development of strategies, actions and tools to strengthen the organisational culture with high ethical standards and to embrace a risk-based approach preventing reputational damage and the sanctioning of its officials. The integrity co-ordinator is trained by the National Directorate for Civil Service and its functions include:

- Implementing actions that promote best practices and update the code of ethics, encouraging ethical thinking in the institution's officials.
- Co-ordinating the implementation of the necessary programmes to disseminate and instruct public officials on the integrity.
- Reporting to the head of the entity and to the integrity committee on the activities, identifying progress in view of generating institutional credibility and trust.
- Disseminating the code of ethics and related material on the entity's webpage and other means used to communicate with its officials.

A key element of the integrity ecosystem in Peru is the so-called 'integrity model and integrity function' that every public entity must implement, regardless of the level of government. Legislative Decree No. 1327 of January 6, 2017, first established the creation of 'Offices of Institutional Integrity' (*Oficinas de integridad institucional*, or OII), whose role was further enhanced by the National Plan of Integrity and Fight Against Corruption and detailed in Resolution No. 1-2019-PCM/SIP. This Resolution from the

Secretariat for Public Integrity makes it mandatory for all the entities to establish an integrity function – to be performed by the OII, the highest administrative authority or the human resources unit department – with the following responsibilities:

- The implementation of the integrity model established in the National Plan and consisting of 9 components (commitment of the senior leadership; risk management; integrity policies; transparency, open data and accountability; internal and external control and audit; communication and training; complaint channels; oversight and monitoring of the integrity model; an official in charge of the integrity model.

- The development of mechanisms and instruments for the promotion of integrity.

- The observance and internalisation of the values and principles linked with the proper use of funds, resources, assets and public responsibilities.

Source: (National Directorate of the Civil Service of Chile, n.d.[41]); (OECD, 2019[50]).

4 Proposals for action to develop integrity systems in Ecuador

This Chapter provides an overview of the actions proposed in the report divided into two parts. The first table includes the recommendations aimed at laying the foundations of a public integrity system at the national level through greater co-operation and a strategic vision. The second table reports the recommendations related to the institutional arrangements for integrity within the Executive branch and its entities, where the role of preventive actors could be recognised and enhanced. For each recommendation, the tables clarify the responsible actors(s) and, when relevant, the envisaged execution term.

The report has analysed the institutional arrangements for integrity at the national level and within the Executive branch of Ecuador in light of the first pillar of the *OECD Recommendation on Public Integrity*. Based on this analysis, it provided recommendations which aim to support Ecuador in institutionalising public integrity and a preventive approach to corruption through institutional co-operation and a strategic approach generating a vision for the country. While these are priority issues and crucial elements to lay the foundations of a public integrity system in Ecuador, additional efforts are needed to build a culture of integrity - both in the public sector and in the society as a whole - and to ensure effective accountability in line with the second and third pillars of the *OECD Recommendation on Public Integrity*.

Table 4.1. Overview of the key recommendations to lay the foundations of a national integrity system

Recommendation	Actor in charge	Execution term
Establish as the first priority objective on public integrity in the National Development Plan 2021-2025 the development of a National Integrity and Anti-corruption System	President of the Republic and National Planning Council	Short term
Initiate a dialogue phase among all relevant actors, including civil society and the private sector to discuss proposals and priorities in shaping the National Integrity and Anti-corruption System.	President of the Republic with support from all relevant branches, especially the Executive and the Transparency and Social Control ones	Short term
Adopt a Law creating the National Integrity and Anti-corruption System	Legislative branch	Short to medium term
Lead and preside the National Integrity and Anti-corruption System	President of the Republic	Not applicable
Take actively part and co-operate in the National Integrity and Anti-corruption System	All institutions which are part to the National Integrity and Anti-corruption System	Not applicable
Establish as the second priority objective on public integrity in the National Development Plan 2021-2025 the development of a National Integrity and Anti-corruption Strategy through a phased roadmap	President of the Republic and National Planning Council	Short term
As first phase, co-ordinate the development of an Action Plan to implement key priority actions of the National Public Integrity and Anti-corruption Plan 2019-2023 while ensuring the involvement of all branches of the State in its design and implementation	National Integrity and Anti-corruption System	Short term
As second phase, co-ordinate the development of a new National Integrity and Anti-corruption Strategy for the 2023-2026 term through a participative and inclusive process which includes civil society organisations and private sector actors	National Integrity and Anti-corruption System	Medium term
Co-ordinate the development and implementation of the National Integrity and Anti-corruption Strategy´s Action Plan 2023-24	National Integrity and Anti-corruption System	Medium term
Co-ordinate the development and implementation of the National Integrity and Anti-corruption Strategy´s Action Plan 2025-26	National Integrity and Anti-corruption System	Medium term
Develop a long-term integrity and anti-corruption state policy	National Planning Council in co-ordination with the National Integrity and Anti-corruption System	Long term

Table 4.2. Overview of the key recommendations to strengthen the institutional arrangements for integrity in the Executive branch

Recommendation	Actor in charge	Execution term
Assign the General Secretariat of the Presidency of the Republic co-ordination and advisory functions on public integrity within the Executive branch as well as the mandate to promote integrity standards and values in public entities of the Executive branch to the Ministry of Labour	President of the Republic	Short term
Lead and co-ordinate the integrity agenda across the entities of the Executive branch and advise the President of the Republic on legal or policy initiatives on integrity and corruption prevention	General Secretariat of the Presidency of the Republic	Not applicable
Within the Executive branch: • Develop, promote and support policies and initiatives aimed at mainstreaming integrity values and standards. • Develop training programmes and arrangements favouring a culture of integrity focused on prevention. • Ensure coherency and co-operate with the General Secretariat of the Presidency of the Republic. • Maintain co-ordination with other entities governing other integrity-related functions or at-risk sectors both in the Executive and Transparency and Social Control branches.	Ministry of Labour	Not applicable
Assign the organisational change and culture units or whoever perform their functions within public institutions and entities of the Executive branch the mandate to promote a preventive approach and a culture of public integrity	Public institutions and entities of the Executive branch	Short term
Within public institutions and entities of the Executive branch: • Support the participatory development of integrity standards. • Provide clarifications and confidential advice on integrity issues. • Organise participative debate and discussions on ethical topics emerging from the advice function and surveys. • Promote and contribute to the capacity building activities on integrity. • Maintain co-ordination with the ethics and anti-bribery committees but also the transparency and open data committees and all the other actors or areas that have relevant responsibilities in relation to human resources, training, transparency, open government, internal control and audit, risk management, investigations, and sanctions.	organisational change and culture units or whoever perform their functions in the public institutions and entities of the Executive branch	Not applicable

References

Anticorruption Alliance of Chile (n.d.), *Participanting entities*,   [38]
http://www.alianzaanticorrupcion.cl/AnticorrupcionUNCAC/sector-publico/# (accessed on
12 April 2021).

Anti-corruption System of Mexico (2020), *Anti-corruption National Policy*,   [28]
https://www.sesna.gob.mx/wp-content/uploads/2020/02/Pol%C3%ADtica-Nacional-
Anticorrupci%C3%B3n.pdf (accessed on 12 April 2021).

CEDATOS (2020), *Political and Electoral Panorama*,   [5]
https://www.cedatos.com.ec/blog/2020/12/07/cedatos-panorama-politico-y-electoral/
(accessed on 25 March 2021).

Charron, N. et al. (2017), "Careers, Connections, and Corruption Risks: Investigating the Impact   [32]
of Bureaucratic Meritocracy on Public Procurement Processes", *The Journal of Politics*,
Vol. 79/1, pp. 89-104, http://dx.doi.org/10.1086/687209.

Council for Citizen Participation and Social Control of Ecuador (2016), *Model for Transparent*   [17]
and Participatory Territories. Guide for Implementation.,
http://www.cpccs.gob.ec/docs/modelo-final.pdf (accessed on 27 March 2021).

Dahlström, C., V. Lapuente and J. Teorell (2012), *The Merit of Meritocratization: Politics,*   [33]
Bureaucracy, and the Institutional Deterrents of Corruption, Sage Publications, Inc.University
of Utah, http://dx.doi.org/10.2307/41635262.

Ecuadorian Standardization Service (n.d.), *The adoption of the ISO 37001 standard will help*   [44]
define anti-corruption strategies, https://www.normalizacion.gob.ec/la-adopcion-de-la-norma-
iso-37001-permitira-definir-estrategias-contra-la-corrupcion/ (accessed on 12 April 2021).

El Comercio (2020), *Secretaría Anticorrupción se suprimió con Decreto 1065*,   [16]
https://www.elcomercio.com/actualidad/secretaria-anticorrupcion-decreto-lenin-moreno.html
(accessed on 25 March 2021).

Front for Transparency and the Fight against Corruption (2017), *Proposals*,   [14]
https://www.cenae.org/uploads/8/2/7/0/82706952/versio%CC%81n_final_151017_propuestas
_finales_ftlc.pdf (accessed on 12 April 2021).

Government of Argentina (2019), *Anti-corruption National Plan 2019-2023*,   [27]
https://www.argentina.gob.ar/sites/default/files/anexo_plan_nacional_anticorrupcion.pdf
(accessed on 12 April 2021).

Government of Paraguay (2020), *National Integrity, Transparency and Anti-corruption Plan 2021-2025*, https://nube.senac.gov.py/s/jRWRXY6nH8iKmMx#pdfviewer (accessed on 12 April 2021). [29]

Government of Peru (2017), *National Integrity and Anti-corruption Policy*, https://cdn.www.gob.pe/uploads/document/file/45986/Politica-Nacional-de-Integridad-y-Lucha-contra-la-Corrupcio%CC%81n.pdf (accessed on 12 April 2021). [30]

Maesschalck, J. and J. Bertok (2009), "Towards a Sound Integrity Framework: Instruments, Processes, Structures and Conditions for Implementation", *SSRN Electronic Journal*, http://dx.doi.org/10.2139/ssrn.2652177. [36]

Meyer-Sahling, J. and K. Mikkelsen (2016), "Civil Service Laws, merit, politicization, and corruption: The perspective of public officials from five East European countries", *Public Administration*, Vol. 94/4, pp. 1105-1123, http://dx.doi.org/10.1111/padm.12276. [34]

Ministerial Advisory Commission for Administrative Probity and Transparency in the Civil Service of Chile; National Directorate of the Civil Service of Chile; (2018), *Ordinance 2305 of 2018*, https://www.gobiernosantiago.cl/wp-content/uploads/2019/12/Oficio-2304-2018-MINSEGPRES.pdf (accessed on 12 April 2021). [39]

Ministry of Economy and Finance of Ecuador (2019), *Standards on the Fight against Corruption and the Anti-bribery Management System in the Ministry of Economy and Finance*, https://www.finanzas.gob.ec/wp-content/uploads/downloads/2019/07/Acuerdo-Lucha-Contra-la-Corrupci%C3%B3n.pdf (accessed on 12 April 2021). [45]

Ministry of Education of Ecuador (2014), *General Coordination for Strategic Management*, https://educacion.gob.ec/wp-content/uploads/downloads/2014/03/7.-COORDINACION-GRAL.-DE-GESTION-ESTRATEGICA.pdf (accessed on 12 April 2021). [49]

Ministry of Health of Ecuador (2012), *Code of Ethics for Good Living of the Executive branch*, https://issuu.com/saludecuador/docs/doc_codigo_etica (accessed on 12 April 2021). [42]

Ministry of Health of Ecuador (n.d.), *What does the National Directorate for Organizational Culture Change do?*. [48]

Ministry of Labour of Ecuador (2018), *Process-based Organic Statute*, https://www.trabajo.gob.ec/wp-content/uploads/2019/03/ESTATUTO-MINISTERIO-DEL-TRABAJO-29112018.pdf (accessed on 26 March 2021). [35]

Moncagatta, P. et al. (2020), *The Political Culture of Democracy in Ecuador and in the Americas, 2018/2019: Taking the Pulse of Democracy*, https://www.vanderbilt.edu/lapop/ecuador/AB2018-19-Ecuador-Country-Report-Eng-V2-W-200903.pdf (accessed on 25 March 2021). [3]

Murphy, J. (2019), "The ISO 37001 Anti-Corruption Compliance Program Standard: What's Good, What's Bad, and Why It Matters", *SSRN Electronic Journal*, http://dx.doi.org/10.2139/ssrn.3315737. [47]

Murtin, F. et al. (2018), "Trust and its determinants: Evidence from the Trustlab experiment", *OECD Statistics Working Papers*, No. 2, https://doi.org/10.1787/869ef2ec-en. [7]

National Assembly of Ecuador (2018), *Organic Law for the Prevention and Eradication of Violence against Women*, https://www.iqualdad.gob.ec/wp-content/uploads/downloads/2018/05/ley_prevenir_y_erradicar_violencia_mujeres.pdf (accessed on 12 April 2021).   [18]

National Assembly of Ecuador (2010), *Planning and Public Finance Organic Code*, https://www.gob.ec/sites/default/files/regulations/2020-06/C%C3%93DIGO_ORG%C3%81NICO_DE_PLANIFICACI%C3%93N_Y_FINANZAS%20-%20diciembre%202019.pdf (accessed on 12 April 2021).   [22]

National Assembly of Ecuador (2008), *Constitution of Ecuador*, https://www.asambleanacional.gob.ec/sites/default/files/documents/old/constitucion_de_bolsillo.pdf (accessed on 12 April 2021).   [13]

National Assembly of Ecuador (2008), *Organic Law of the National Public Procurement System*, https://portal.compraspublicas.gob.ec/sercop/wp-content/uploads/2018/10/LOSNCP-ultima.pdf (accessed on 12 April 2021).   [19]

National Directorate of the Civil Service of Chile (n.d.), *Integrity Systems and Code of Ethics*, https://www.serviciocivil.cl/sistemas-de-integridad-y-codigo-de-etica/ (accessed on 12 April 2021).   [41]

National Directorate of the Civil Service of Chile; Comptroller General Office of Chile (2017), *Probity and Public Ethics. Legal Framework*, https://documentos.serviciocivil.cl/actas/dnsc/documentService/downloadWs?uuid=482d8510-6961-4872-a000-ebfdc2f6f9e9 (accessed on 12 April 2021).   [40]

OECD (2020), *OECD Public Integrity Handbook*, OECD Publishing, Paris, https://dx.doi.org/10.1787/ac8ed8e8-en.   [12]

OECD (2019), *La Integridad Pública en América Latina y el Caribe 2018-2019*, OECD, Paris, http://www.oecd.org/gov/integridad/integridad-publica-en-america-latina-caribe-2018-2019.htm (accessed on 25 February 2020).   [1]

OECD (2019), *Offices of Institutional Integrity in Peru: Implementing the Integrity System*, OECD, Paris, http://www.oecd.org/gov/ethics/offices-of-institutional-integrity-peru.pdf.   [50]

OECD (2017), *OECD Integrity Review of Peru: Enhancing Public Sector Integrity for Inclusive Growth*, OECD Public Governance Reviews, OECD Publishing, Paris, https://dx.doi.org/10.1787/9789264271029-en.   [46]

OECD (2017), *OECD Recommendation on Public Integrity*, OECD, Paris, http://www.oecd.org/gov/ethics/Recommendation-Public-Integrity.pdf (accessed on 6 July 2017).   [6]

OECD (2010), *Recommendation of the Council on Principles for Transparency and Integrity in Lobbying*, OECD, Paris, https://legalinstruments.oecd.org/Instruments/ShowInstrumentView.aspx?InstrumentID=256&   [9]

OECD (2004), "OECD Guidelines for Managing Conflict of Interest in the Public Service", in *Managing Conflict of Interest in the Public Service: OECD Guidelines and Country Experiences*, OECD Publishing, Paris, https://dx.doi.org/10.1787/9789264104938-2-en.   [8]

OECD (n.d.), *About the OECD*, https://www.oecd.org/about/ (accessed on 12 April 2021).   [11]

OECD (forthcoming), *Multi-Dimensional Review of Ecuador*. [4]

OECD (n.d.), "Public Integrity in Latin America and the Caribbean", [10]
https://www.oecd.org/governance/ethics/integrity-lac.htm (accessed on 12 April 2021).

OECD et al. (2019), *Latin American Economic Outlook 2019: Development in Transition*, OECD [2]
Publishing, Paris, https://dx.doi.org/10.1787/g2g9ff18-en.

Open Government Ecuador (2019), *Open Government Action Plan of Ecuador 2019-2022*, [26]
https://www.opengovpartnership.org/wp-content/uploads/2020/01/Ecuador_Action-
Plan_2019-2021.pdf (accessed on 12 April 2021).

PADF; FCD; CSIS (2020), *Diagnóstico sobre áreas prioritarias para la cooperación contra la* [15]
corrupción en Ecuador, https://padf.org/wp-content/uploads/2020/09/Informe-de-consultoria-
con-portada.pdf (accessed on 12 February 2021).

Presidency of the Republic of Ecuador (2019), *2019 Annual Address of the President to the* [43]
Nation, https://www.presidencia.gob.ec/wp-content/uploads/downloads/2019/05/2019.05.24-
INFORME-A-LA-NACI%C3%93N.pdf (accessed on 12 April 2021).

Presidency of the Republic of Ecuador (2016), *Decree 1067 of 8 June 2016*, [37]
https://www.presidencia.gob.ec/wp-
content/uploads/downloads/2016/07/a1_decreto_1067.pdf (accessed on 12 April 2021).

Pyman, M., S. Eastwood and J. Elliott (2017), *Research comparing 41 national anti-corruption* [24]
strategies: Insights and guidance for leaders, Norton Rose Fulbright,
http://www.nortonrosefulbright.com/knowledge/publications/147479/countries-
curbingcorruption.

Technical Secretariat Planifica Ecuador (2019), *Technical Standard of the National System for* [31]
Participative Planning, https://www.planificacion.gob.ec/wp-
content/uploads/downloads/2019/12/Norma_Tecnica_del_Sistema_Nacional_de_Planificacio
n_Participativa.pdf (accessed on 27 March 2021).

Transparency and Social Control Function of Ecuador (2019), *National Public Integrity and* [21]
Anticorruption Plan 2019-2023,
https://www.contraloria.gob.ec/WFDescarga.aspx?id=2629&tipo=doc (accessed on
19 February 2021).

UNDOC (2020), *Second Review Cycle of the UNCAC: Answers from autoevaluation* [20]
questionnaire of Ecuador.

UNDP (2014), *Anti-corruption Strategies: Understanding what works, what doesn't and why?* [25]
Lessons learned from the Asia-Pacific Region, United Nations Development Programme,
New York, https://www.undp.org/content/undp/en/home/librarypage/democratic-
governance/anti-corruption/Report.html (accessed on 27 March 2021).

UNODC (2015), *National Anti-Corruption Strategies: A Practical Guide for Development and* [23]
Implementation, United Nations Office on Drugs and Crime, New York,
https://www.unodc.org/documents/corruption/Publications/2015/National_Anti-
Corruption_Strategies_-_A_Practical_Guide_for_Development_and_Implementation_E.pdf
(accessed on 7 January 2018).

Lightning Source UK Ltd.
Milton Keynes UK
UKHW050238060721
386670UK00002B/10